THE ULTIMATE GUIDE TO MAKING MONEY ONLINE:

DETAILED GUILDE TO
THE SECRETS OF
FINANCIAL FREEDOM

JOSEPH WEALTH

COPYRIGHT

TABLE OF CONTENTS

INTRODUCTION

The Ultimate Guide to Making Money Online is a comprehensive resource that provides practical tips and strategies for earning income on the internet. In today's digital age, there are countless opportunities to leverage technology and the internet to generate income, whether through freelance work, entrepreneurship, e-commerce, affiliate marketing, or other methods.

This guide is designed to help individuals who are looking to earn additional income or start a business online by providing actionable steps and insights. It covers a range of topics including how to identify profitable niches, how to create and market digital products, how to monetize a blog or website, and how to leverage social media platforms to grow an online business.

Whether you are a beginner looking to start your first online business or an experienced entrepreneur seeking to expand your digital footprint, this guide provides valuable information and resources to help you succeed in the fast-paced and ever-evolving world of online business.

Making money online has become increasingly popular in recent years, thanks to the growth of the internet and the rise of the gig economy. Whether you're looking to make a little extra cash on the side or want to start a full-time online business, there are countless opportunities available to you. Here's an ultimate guide to making money online:

1. Freelancing: Freelancing is one of the most popular ways to make money online. You can offer your services as a writer, designer, developer, social media manager, or any other skill you have. You can find freelance work on websites like Upwork, Freelancer, and Fiverr.

2. Online surveys: You can get paid for taking online surveys for companies that want to know what their customers think. Websites like

Swagbucks, Survey Junkie, and InboxDollars pay you for completing surveys.

3. Online tutoring: If you have expertise in a particular subject, you can offer online tutoring services to students. You can find tutoring jobs on websites like Tutor.com and Chegg.

4. Affiliate marketing: Affiliate marketing involves promoting other people's products and earning a commission for each sale you make. You can sign up for affiliate programs on websites like Amazon Associates, Clickbank, and Commission Junction.

5. E-commerce: E-commerce involves selling products online. You can create your own online store on websites like Shopify or sell on marketplaces like Amazon and eBay.

6. Blogging: Blogging involves creating content on a particular topic and making money through advertising, affiliate marketing, or selling products. You can create your own blog using platforms like WordPress or Blogger.

7. Online courses: If you have expertise in a particular area, you can create and sell online courses on websites like Udemy and Skillshare.

8. Virtual assistant: You can offer administrative services to businesses and individuals as a virtual assistant. You can find virtual assistant jobs on websites like Zirtual and Upwork.

9. YouTube: You can make money on YouTube by creating and monetizing your own videos. You can earn money through advertising revenue, sponsorships, and merchandise sales.

10. Online gaming: If you're a skilled gamer, you can make money by streaming your gameplay on platforms like Twitch and YouTube. You can earn money through advertising revenue, sponsorships, and donations.

There are countless other ways to make money online, but these are some of the most popular and accessible. The key is to find something that you enjoy and are good at, and then work hard to build your audience and your income.

REASON TO BE DIGITALLY AWARE IN THIS PRESENCE WORLD

In today's world, being digitally aware is essential for a variety of reasons, including:

1. Communication: Digital communication has become a dominant mode of communication in our daily lives. Being digitally aware helps us to communicate effectively using digital tools such as emails, instant messaging, and social media.

2. Information access: The internet has made it easier for people to access vast amounts of information on any subject. Being digitally aware allows us to navigate the web and find relevant information quickly and efficiently.

3. Online safety: With the rise of online scams, cyberbullying, and identity theft, being digitally

aware is crucial to protect ourselves and our personal information from online threats.

4. Career opportunities: Many jobs today require digital skills, and being digitally aware is a necessity to compete in the job market. Digital literacy is no longer an added bonus but a basic requirement for most job positions.

5. Digital citizenship: Being digitally aware means being a responsible digital citizen who uses digital tools responsibly and ethically, respecting others' privacy and intellectual property rights.

In summary, being digitally aware is essential to succeed in today's digital world. It allows us to communicate effectively, access information, stay safe online, explore career opportunities, and be responsible digital citizens.

HOW THE INTERNET HAS OPENED UP A WORLD OF OPPORTUNITIES

The internets have revolutionized the way we live, work, and communicate, opening up a world of opportunities for people all over the globe. Here are some ways in which the internet has created new opportunities:

1. Access to information: The internet has made information readily available to people worldwide. With just a few clicks, you can access a wealth of information on any topic you are interested in, from history to science, from fashion to business, and much more. This has democratized knowledge and created new opportunities for people to learn and explore.

2. E-commerce: The internet has enabled people to buy and sell goods and services online, creating a new wave of entrepreneurs and small business owners. With the rise of e-commerce platforms, people can start their own online stores and

reach customers around the world, without the need for a physical storefront.

3. Remote work: The internet has enabled people to work remotely, opening up opportunities for people who may not have access to traditional employment. Remote work has allowed people to work from anywhere, as long as they have an internet connection, which has been especially helpful for people who live in rural areas or have disabilities.

4. Social media: Social media has created new opportunities for people to connect with others and build their personal brands. With social media, people can promote their work, share their ideas, and connect with people from all over the world, creating new opportunities for networking and collaboration.

5. Online education: The internet has made education more accessible to people all over the world, with the rise of online courses, webinars, and other educational resources. This has

created new opportunities for people to learn new skills and advance their careers, regardless of their location or background.

Overall, the internet has opened up a world of opportunities, empowering people to connect, learn, and create in ways that were once impossible.

Chapter One

CHAPTER ONE

UNDERSTANDING THE ONLINE MARKETPLACE

The online marketplace refers to a digital platform that enables buyers and sellers to engage in commercial transactions over the internet. It provides an avenue for businesses of all sizes to showcase their products and services to a broader audience beyond their physical location.

In an online marketplace, buyers can search for and purchase products from various sellers, while sellers can list their products for sale and receive payment for them. Online marketplaces provide a level playing field for businesses of all sizes to compete and reach customers across the globe.

Online marketplaces can be divided into two categories: horizontal and vertical. Horizontal marketplaces are those that offer a wide range of products from different categories, while vertical marketplaces specialize in specific product categories or niches.

Examples of popular online marketplaces include Amazon, eBay, Alibaba, Etsy, and Uber. Each of these platforms has unique features, rules, and regulations that govern how buyers and sellers interact and transact.

To succeed in an online marketplace, sellers need to have a deep understanding of their target audience, competitors, and the platform's policies. They also need to optimize their product listings with high-quality images, accurate descriptions, and competitive pricing.

On the other hand, buyers need to be cautious and conduct due diligence before making purchases. They should read product reviews, check the seller's reputation, and ensure that their personal and financial information is secure before making any transactions.

In summary, the online marketplace provides a convenient and accessible platform for businesses and consumers to connect and engage in commerce. However, success in the online marketplace requires both sellers and buyers to understand the platform's rules and regulations, as well as best practices for conducting transactions.

WHAT ARE THE THINGS TO UNDERSTAND IN THE ONLINE MARKETPLACE

Here are some things to understand about the online marketplace:

1. Competition: The online marketplace is a highly competitive environment, and you will be competing with other businesses that sell similar products or services. It's important to differentiate your business from others and find ways to stand out.

2. Target audience: Knowing your target audience is essential in the online marketplace. You need

to understand their needs, interests, and behaviors to tailor your marketing efforts and product offerings.

3. Platform selection: There are numerous platforms available for selling products and services online. You need to choose the platform that suits your business needs and audience preferences. Each platform has its own features, fees, and policies.

4. Marketing strategies: Developing effective marketing strategies is crucial for attracting and retaining customers in the online marketplace. You can use a combination of search engine optimization (SEO), social media marketing, email marketing, content marketing, and paid advertising.

5. Payment and shipping options: Providing secure and convenient payment and shipping options is important for customer satisfaction. You need to select reliable payment gateways and shipping

providers and provide clear information about shipping times and costs.

6. Customer service: Providing excellent customer service is essential for building a loyal customer base. You need to respond to customer inquiries promptly and address any issues or concerns in a professional and timely manner.

7. Legal requirements: There are legal requirements for selling products and services online, such as registering your business, obtaining necessary licenses and permits, complying with tax laws, and protecting customers' privacy and data. You need to ensure that you are complying with all applicable laws and regulations.

THE RISE AND IMPORTANCE OF E-COMMERCE

E-commerce, or electronic commerce, refers to the buying and selling of goods and services over the internet. It has become a significant aspect of modern-day business, and its rise in popularity has transformed the way people shop and conduct transactions.

The rise of e-commerce can be traced back to the early 1990s, when the first online marketplace was established. Since then, the popularity of e-commerce has skyrocketed, driven by the growth of the internet, the increasing availability of affordable technology, and the convenience it offers to both consumers and businesses.

One of the primary reasons for the rise of e-commerce is the convenience it provides. Customers can shop for products from anywhere, at any time, using any device with an internet connection. This has made it easier for consumers to find and purchase products that may not be available in their local stores. E-commerce has also allowed businesses to reach a wider audience, expanding their customer base beyond their geographic location.

Another factor contributing to the growth of e-commerce is the rise of mobile devices. The proliferation of smartphones and tablets has made it even easier for consumers to shop online, as they can do so from virtually anywhere. This has also led to the rise of mobile commerce, or m-commerce, where customers can make purchases directly from their mobile devices.

E-commerce has also had a significant impact on the global economy. It has allowed small businesses to compete with larger ones on a more level playing field, as they can reach a wider audience without the need for a physical storefront. Additionally, e-commerce has created new job opportunities in areas such as website design, logistics, and customer service.

In summary, the rise of e-commerce has transformed the way people shop and do business. It has provided customers with greater convenience, allowed businesses to reach a wider audience, and had a significant impact on the global economy. As technology continues to evolve, it is likely that e-commerce will continue to play an increasingly important role in the way we conduct transactions.

The rise of e-commerce has been one of the most significant developments in the business world in recent decades. E-commerce refers to the buying and selling of goods and services over the internet, and it has completely transformed the way that many businesses operate. Here are some of the key factors that have contributed to the rise of e-commerce:

1. Increasing Internet Penetration: One of the most critical factors that have contributed to the rise of e-commerce is the increasing availability of the internet. As internet access has become more widespread, more people are now able to shop online.

2. Improved Mobile Connectivity: Another factor that has contributed to the rise of e-commerce is the proliferation of mobile devices. With the increasing popularity of smartphones and

tablets, people are now able to shop online from anywhere at any time.

3. Convenience and Accessibility: Online shopping offers a level of convenience and accessibility that traditional brick-and-mortar stores simply cannot match. Customers can shop from the comfort of their own homes and have products delivered directly to their doorsteps.

4. Lower Overhead Costs: E-commerce businesses typically have lower overhead costs compared to traditional brick-and-mortar stores. Online businesses don't need to pay rent for a physical storefront, and they don't need to hire as many employees to manage their operations.

5. Global Reach: E-commerce businesses have a much wider reach compared to traditional brick-and-mortar stores. With the internet, businesses can easily reach customers all over the world, making it possible to tap into new markets and expand their customer base.

6. Technological Advances: The development of new technologies such as online payment systems, data analytics, and artificial intelligence has also contributed to the rise of e-commerce.

THE GIG ECONOMY AND IT IMPORTANCE

The gig economy refers to a labor market where individuals work on a temporary, part-time, or freelance basis, often for multiple clients or employers. The term "gig" originally referred to musical performances, but it has since expanded to include a wide range of jobs, such as driving for ride-sharing companies, delivering food, providing online services like programming and design, and more.

The gig economy has become increasingly important in recent years for several reasons. First, it offers greater flexibility for workers, who can choose when and where they work, and often have control over their own schedules. This can be particularly beneficial for people with other commitments, such as caregiving responsibilities or students who need to balance work and school.

Second, the gig economy can provide a source of income for people who may have difficulty finding traditional employment, such as those with disabilities or who live in rural areas with limited job opportunities.

Third, the gig economy can benefit businesses by allowing them to access a pool of skilled workers on an as-needed basis, without the expense of hiring full-time employees.

However, the gig economy has also faced criticism for its potential to exploit workers, who may not have access to benefits such as health insurance or retirement plans, and may be subject to unpredictable income streams. Additionally, the lack of regulations and protections for gig workers can make it difficult for them to advocate for their rights.

Overall, the gig economy is an important part of the modern labor market, offering both benefits and challenges for workers, businesses, and society as a whole.

THE IMPORTANCE OF BUILDING A PERSONAL BRAND

Building a personal brand is increasingly important in today's digital age, where your online presence can have a significant impact on your personal and professional life. A personal brand is the image and reputation that you create for yourself, based on your skills, expertise, and values. Here are some reasons why building a personal brand is crucial:

1. Stand Out from the Crowd: In a highly competitive job market, having a strong personal brand can help you stand out from the competition. It enables you to differentiate yourself and showcase your unique skills and expertise, which can attract potential employers and clients.

2. Build Credibility and Trust: A well-crafted personal brand can help establish your credibility and build trust with your audience. When you consistently deliver valuable content

and engage with your followers, you create a loyal fan base that believes in your message and expertise.

3. Increase Visibility: Building a personal brand can help increase your visibility and reach. By creating content and sharing it across different channels, you can increase your online presence and attract a wider audience.

4. Expand Your Network: A strong personal brand can also help you expand your professional network. By establishing yourself as an authority in your field, you can attract other like-minded individuals who can help you grow your business or advance your career.

5. Create New Opportunities: A well-established personal brand can open up new opportunities that you may not have otherwise considered. You may be invited to speak at conferences, collaborate on projects, or even be approached for media opportunities.

In summary, building a personal brand is essential for anyone who wants to stand out in today's digital age. By creating a strong online presence and showcasing your skills and expertise, you can establish credibility, build trust, increase your visibility, expand your network, and create new opportunities for growth and success.

THE HOLISTICALLY WAYS TO BUILDING A PERSONAL BRAND THAT WORKS

Building a personal brand is a process of establishing a unique and authentic identity for yourself in the public domain. It involves creating a strong reputation, a clear voice, and a consistent image that represents who you are and what you stand for. Here's a holistic overview of how building a personal brand works:

1. Define Your Personal Brand: The first step in building a personal brand is to define who you are, what you do, and what makes you unique.

Identify your strengths, skills, values, and passions that set you apart from others.

2. Create Your Brand Identity: Once you have defined your personal brand, you need to create a brand identity that represents you. This includes developing a brand name, tagline, logo, and visual style that align with your personal brand.

3. Build Your Online Presence: In today's digital age, having a strong online presence is essential for building a personal brand. Create profiles on social media platforms like LinkedIn, Twitter, and Instagram, and create a personal website or blog to showcase your expertise and achievements.

4. Develop Your Voice: Your voice is the way you communicate your personal brand to others. Develop a clear, consistent, and authentic voice that reflects your values, personality, and expertise.

5. Establish Your Reputation: Building a personal brand requires developing a positive reputation in your industry or field. Build relationships with other professionals, seek out speaking opportunities, and share your expertise through content creation and thought leadership.

6. Maintain Your Brand: Building a personal brand is an ongoing process. Continuously assess your brand, monitor your online presence, and adapt your strategy as needed to ensure that your brand stays relevant and authentic.

In summary, building a personal brand is a holistic process that requires defining your personal brand, creating a brand identity, building an online presence, developing your voice, establishing your reputation, and maintaining your brand over time. By following these steps, you can create a strong and authentic personal brand that reflects who you are and what you stand for.

HOLISTICALLY APPROACH TO BRANDING

A holistic approach to branding involves considering all aspects of a brand and how they work together to create a unified and cohesive image. This approach considers all touchpoints with customers, from visual elements like logos and packaging, to messaging, customer service, and even the company's values and mission.

Here are some key elements to consider when taking a holistic approach to branding:

1. Brand Identity: Your brand identity includes the visual elements that customers associate with your brand, such as logos, color schemes, typography, and packaging design. These elements should be consistent across all channels and should communicate the essence of your brand.

2. Brand Messaging: Your brand messaging includes the words and language you use to

communicate your brand's personality, values, and benefits to customers. This should be consistent across all channels and should resonate with your target audience.

3. Customer Experience: Your brand should provide a seamless and enjoyable experience for customers at all touch points, from browsing your website to interacting with customer service. Every interaction with your brand should reinforce your messaging and identity.

4. Brand Values: Your brand's values and mission should be clearly communicated and demonstrated through your actions as a company. This can include social responsibility initiatives or commitment to sustainability.

5. Brand Strategy: Your brand strategy should align with your overall business goals and should take into account market research and customer insights to guide decision-making.

By taking a holistic approach to branding, you can create a consistent and compelling brand image that resonates with customers and helps differentiate your company from competitors.

Chapter Two

CHAPTER TWO

WHAT IS FREELANCING

Freelancing is a type of self-employment where an individual offers their skills and services to clients on a project-by-project basis, rather than being employed by a company on a full-time or long-term basis. Freelancers work independently and are typically not bound by a contract, allowing them the freedom to take on multiple clients and projects at once.

Freelancing is commonly associated with creative and technical professions, such as writing, graphic design, web development, and programming, but it can also be applied to a wide range of industries and services.

Freelancers are responsible for finding and securing their own clients, negotiating their own rates, and managing their own schedules and workload. They may work from home, a co-working space, or any location with an internet connection. Freelancing can offer flexibility, autonomy, and the potential for higher earning potential, but it also requires discipline, self-motivation, and the ability to manage multiple projects simultaneously.

WHAT IS CONSULTING FREELANCING

Consulting freelancing refers to the practice of providing consulting services to clients as an independent contractor, rather than as an employee of a consulting firm or other organization. As a freelance consultant, you work for yourself and can choose your clients and projects, set your own rates and work schedule, and take full responsibility for delivering the agreed-upon services.

Consulting freelancing can involve providing a wide range of services, such as business strategy consulting, marketing and advertising, financial analysis, IT consulting, and human resources consulting, among others. Freelance consultants may work with a variety of clients, including startups, small businesses, non-profit organizations, and larger corporations.

To be successful as a consulting freelancer, you will need to have expertise in a particular area, excellent communication skills, and the ability to manage your own workload and prioritize tasks effectively. You will also need to be comfortable with self-promotion and marketing your services to potential clients.

FREELANCING AND CONSULTING

FREELANCING AND CONSULTING

Freelancing and consulting are two popular ways for professionals to offer their services to clients on a project-by-project basis. While both involve working independently, there are some key differences between the two.

Freelancing typically involves working as a self-employed individual and offering your services to clients on a project-by-project basis. Freelancers are usually responsible for finding their own clients, setting their own rates, and managing their own workload. They may work on a variety of projects for multiple clients at the same time, and may specialize in a particular area such as writing, design, or programming.

Consulting, on the other hand, typically involves providing expert advice and guidance to clients on a specific topic or problem. Consultants are often hired by businesses or organizations to help them improve their operations, increase efficiency, or solve complex problems. Consultants typically work on a project-by-project basis, but their focus is more on providing strategic guidance and expertise rather than completing specific tasks.

Both freelancing and consulting offer professionals the flexibility to work on their own terms, choose their own clients and projects, and set their own rates. However, consulting typically requires a higher level of expertise and specialized knowledge, while freelancing may involve a broader range of skills and projects.

MAKING THROUGH FREELANCING AND CONSULTING FREELANCING

Freelancing refers to working as a self-employed individual and offering services to clients on a project or hourly basis. The services can range from writing, graphic designing, web development, social media management, virtual assistance, and more.

One of the advantages of freelancing is that you have control over your rates and work schedule. As you gain experience and build a portfolio, you can increase your rates and attract more high-paying clients. Freelancing also provides flexibility, allowing you to work from anywhere as long as you have a reliable internet connection.

To start freelancing, you need to identify your skills and niche, build a portfolio, and create a profile on freelancing platforms such as Upwork, Fiverr, and Freelancer. You can also reach out to potential clients through social media platforms or your network.

Consulting, on the other hand, involves providing expert advice to businesses and organizations on specific areas such as marketing, finance, HR, and more. As a consultant, you will be expected to have extensive knowledge and experience in your field of expertise.

Consulting fees can be higher than freelance rates, but it requires a higher level of expertise and a more comprehensive understanding of the business environment. To become a consultant, you need to have a solid understanding of your field, build a professional network, and have a proven track record of delivering results.

To get started in consulting, you can network with professionals in your field, join consulting firms, or start your consulting business. You can also create content such as blog posts and videos to establish yourself as an expert in your field.

In conclusion, freelancing and consulting are great ways to make money while working for yourself. With dedication and hard work, you can build a successful career in either of these fields.

HOW TO GET STARTED AS A FREELANCER OR CONSULTANT

Getting started as a freelancer or consultant can be challenging, but with the right approach, you can successfully launch your business. Here are some steps to get started:

1. Identify your skills and expertise: Determine what skills and expertise you have to offer as a freelancer or consultant. Consider your experience, education, and certifications, and choose a niche that aligns with your interests and strengths.

2. Define your services: Identify the services you will offer as a freelancer or consultant. Think about what problems you can solve for clients

and what services they will be willing to pay for.

3. Build a portfolio: As a new freelancer or consultant, you may not have many clients or projects to showcase. But you can create a portfolio of your work by completing sample projects or working on small projects for friends or family.

4. Set your pricing: Determine your pricing structure based on your expertise, the market rate for your services, and your target audience's ability to pay. Start with competitive pricing to build your client base and increase your rates over time.

5. Market your services: Use social media, networking, and word-of-mouth referrals to promote your services. Create a website or portfolio to showcase your work and make it easy for potential clients to contact you.

6. Deliver quality work: Once you have landed your first client, make sure to deliver high-

quality work and exceed their expectations. This will help you build a good reputation and get more referrals in the future.

7. Continuously learn and improve: As a freelancer or consultant, it is important to continuously learn and improve your skills to stay competitive in the market. Attend webinars, workshops, and conferences related to your niche, and seek feedback from clients to improve your services.

Remember that building a successful freelance or consulting business takes time and effort. Be patient, persistent, and always deliver your best work to your clients.

HOW TO MAKE MONEY THROUGH FREELANCING AND CONSULTING FREELANCING

There are several ways to make money through freelancing and consulting. Here are some tips to help you get started:

1. Identify your skills: The first step is to identify the skills you have that can be monetized. Look for skills that are in demand and that you enjoy doing.

2. Create a portfolio: A portfolio is a collection of your work that showcases your skills and abilities. It can include examples of your past work, testimonials from previous clients, and any relevant certifications or degrees you have.

3. Set your rates: Determine your hourly or project-based rate. Research what other freelancers in your field are charging to get an idea of what to charge.

4. Find clients: There are several ways to find clients, including online job boards, social media, referrals, and networking events.

5. Build relationships with clients: Once you have clients, focus on building a strong relationship with them. Provide high-quality work, communicate regularly, and be responsive to their needs.

6. Market yourself: As a freelancer, you are your own brand. Make sure you have a professional website and social media presence. Use these platforms to showcase your work, share your expertise, and connect with potential clients.

7. Expand your services: As you gain more experience, consider expanding your services to offer more to your clients. This can help you increase your income and build a stronger relationship with your clients.

8. Stay organized: Freelancing can be unpredictable, so it's important to stay organized. Use tools like calendars, to-do lists,

and project management software to stay on top of your work and deadlines.

By following these tips, you can build a successful freelancing and consulting career and make money doing what you love.

HERE'S A CASE STUDY OF FREELANCING AND CONSULTING FREELANCING:

Case Study:

Sarah is a marketing professional with over a decade of experience in the industry. She decides to leave her corporate job and start her own marketing consultancy business. Sarah knows that starting a consultancy business can be challenging, especially in the initial stages. However, she is confident in her skills and believes that she can make a successful career out of it.

To start her business, Sarah decides to leverage her network and reach out to her existing clients and connections. She also creates a website and social media accounts to promote her services and build her brand.

Initially, Sarah starts by offering her services as a freelance marketer, working on a project-by-project basis for various clients. She sets her rates based on her experience and expertise and communicates them clearly to her clients. Sarah ensures that she is transparent about her services and the timeline for completing projects, to avoid any misunderstandings.

As Sarah works on various projects for her clients, she realizes that there is a need for her services on an ongoing basis. Sarah sees an opportunity to offer her services as a consultant, where she can work with her clients on a long-term basis and provide more comprehensive solutions.

Sarah decides to pivot her business model to focus more on consulting. She begins by identifying her ideal clients and developing a proposal for her services. She communicates the value of her services and the benefits of working with her as a consultant. Sarah also emphasizes the importance of building a strong partnership with her clients, where she can work closely with them to achieve their marketing goals.

With her new focus on consulting, Sarah is able to secure more long-term clients and build stronger relationships with them. She is also able to increase her rates as she is providing more strategic and comprehensive solutions to her clients.

As Sarah continues to grow her business, she invests in building her team and expanding her services. She hires a few freelancers to support her on various projects, allowing her to take on more work and offer more diverse solutions to her clients.

CONCLUSION:

Sarah's case study highlights the potential of freelancing and consulting freelancing as a career path. By leveraging her experience and expertise, Sarah was able to build a successful consultancy business that provided value to her clients. She was able to pivot her business model based on the needs of her clients, which allowed her to offer more comprehensive solutions and build stronger relationships with them. Through her efforts, Sarah was able to build a sustainable and profitable business that provided her with the freedom and flexibility she desired.

HOW TO FIND CLIENTS

Finding clients can be a challenging task for any business, especially if you're just starting out. However, there are several strategies you can use to attract new clients and grow your customer base. Here are some tips on how to find clients:

1. Define your target audience: The first step in finding clients is to determine your target audience. Who are your ideal customers? What are their needs, interests, and pain points? By identifying your target audience, you can tailor your marketing efforts to their specific needs and preferences.

2. Use social media: Social media is a powerful tool for connecting with potential clients. Identify which social media platforms your target audience is most active on and create a presence there. Share valuable content, engage with your followers, and use hashtags to increase your reach.

3. Attend networking events: Attend industry events and conferences to meet potential clients face-to-face. Bring business cards and be prepared to talk about your business and what makes it unique.

4. Offer free consultations or samples: Offering a free consultation or sample of your product or service can be an effective way to attract new clients. This allows potential clients to try your product or service before committing to a purchase.

5. Ask for referrals: Word-of-mouth marketing is a powerful tool for attracting new clients. Ask your existing clients for referrals and offer incentives for each new client they bring in.

6. Partner with complementary businesses: Partnering with businesses that offer complementary products or services can help you reach a wider audience. Look for businesses that share your target audience and offer mutually beneficial partnerships.

7. Create a website: A website is a must-have for any business looking to attract clients online. Make sure your website is optimized for search engines and includes clear calls to action that encourage visitors to contact you.

8. Invest in advertising: Paid advertising can help you reach a wider audience and generate new leads. Consider using Google AdWords, Facebook Ads, or other paid advertising platforms to reach your target audience.

By using these strategies, you can attract new clients and grow your business. However, it's important to remember that finding clients is an ongoing process that requires time and effort. Stay persistent and keep experimenting with new strategies to find what works best for your business.

HOW TO ATTRACT HIGH PAYING CLIENTS

Attracting high-paying clients requires a combination of several factors, including your expertise, your brand reputation, your marketing strategy, and your networking skills. Here are some steps you can take to attract high-paying clients:

1. Define Your Niche and Expertise: To attract high-paying clients, it's essential to establish yourself as an expert in your field. Start by identifying your niche and your area of expertise. What are you best at? What makes you unique and valuable to your clients? What do you offer that others don't? Focus on your core strengths and make sure that you're communicating them clearly to your potential clients.

2. Develop a Strong Brand: Your brand is how people perceive you and your business. A strong brand can help you stand out from the competition and attract high-paying clients. Invest in creating a professional website, business cards, and marketing materials that reflect your expertise and values. Use social

media to showcase your work and engage with potential clients.

3. Build a Portfolio: A strong portfolio is essential to attracting high-paying clients. It's a visual representation of your skills and experience that shows your potential clients what you're capable of. Make sure your portfolio is up-to-date, showcases your best work, and highlights your successes.

4. Network with Influencers: Networking with influencers in your industry can help you gain exposure and build relationships with high-paying clients. Attend industry events, join professional associations, and participate in online communities to connect with influencers and build your reputation.

5. Leverage Your Existing Client Base: Your existing clients can be a valuable source of referrals and testimonials. If you have a track record of delivering quality work and exceptional customer service, your clients may

refer you to others who are willing to pay top dollar for your services.

6. Set Your Prices Appropriately: Setting your prices too low may attract clients who are looking for a bargain, but it won't attract high-paying clients. On the other hand, setting your prices too high may make you appear out of reach. Research your industry's pricing standards and set your prices accordingly.

7. Provide Exceptional Service: High-paying clients expect exceptional service, so make sure you're delivering on your promises. Communicate clearly with your clients, meet deadlines, and go above and beyond to exceed their expectations. Happy clients are more likely to refer you to others and give you repeat business.

In summary, attracting high-paying clients takes effort, but it's worth it. By defining your niche, building a strong brand, networking with influencers, leveraging your existing client base, setting your prices appropriately, and providing exceptional service, you can establish yourself as a valuable expert in your field and attract clients who are willing to pay top dollar for your services.

HOW TO ATTRACT THE RIGHT CLIENTS

Attracting the right clients is essential for the success of any business. Here are some steps you can take to attract the right clients:

1. Define your ideal client: You need to have a clear understanding of the type of clients you want to attract. This includes their age, gender, location, interests, and needs. Once you have this information, you can tailor your marketing messages to attract them.

2. Create a strong brand: Your brand should communicate your values, expertise, and the benefits of working with you. Your website, logo, social media profiles, and marketing

materials should all be consistent and appealing to your ideal clients.

3. Develop a content strategy: Creating valuable content that resonates with your ideal clients can help attract them to your business. This can include blog posts, social media posts, videos, webinars, and podcasts. Make sure your content addresses their pain points, answers their questions, and provides solutions.

4. Build a referral network: Referrals are one of the most effective ways to attract new clients. You can build a referral network by partnering with complementary businesses, offering referral incentives, and asking happy clients for referrals.

5. Use targeted advertising: Advertising can be expensive, so it's important to target your ads to reach the right audience. You can use social media advertising, Google Ads, or other online advertising platforms to target your ideal clients

based on their demographics, interests, and behavior.

6. Attend events and network: Attending industry events and networking with other professionals can help you meet potential clients and build relationships. Make sure to have your elevator pitch ready and bring business cards.

7. Offer value upfront: Offering a free consultation, a free trial, or a lead magnet can help attract potential clients and demonstrate your expertise. Make sure to follow up with them after they've received the value you offered.

Attracting the right clients requires a clear understanding of your ideal client, a strong brand, valuable content, a referral network, targeted advertising, networking, and offering value upfront. By implementing these strategies, you can attract

SETTING YOUR RATES

If you're looking to set your rates, here are some steps you can follow:

1. Research industry standards: Look at what others in your industry are charging for similar services or products. This will give you an idea of what the market is willing to pay.

2. Determine your costs: You need to know how much it costs you to provide your service or product, including any materials, labor, and overhead costs. This will help you ensure that your rates cover your expenses and provide a reasonable profit.

3. Consider your experience and expertise: If you have specialized skills or years of experience, you can charge more for your services than someone just starting out.

4. Decide on your pricing strategy: There are several pricing strategies to choose from, such as flat rate, hourly rate, or project-based.

Consider which one makes the most sense for your business and your clients.

5. Test your rates: Once you have determined your rates, test them out on a few clients to see how they respond. You may need to adjust your rates based on feedback or market demand.

Remember, setting your rates is not a one-time task. You may need to adjust your rates over time as your business grows and your expenses change.

KNOWING THE RIGHT RATES TO SET

The right rates to set depend on the context of what you're referring to. If you're asking about setting rates for a service or product, it's important to consider factors such as the value of the service or product, the competition, and the target market. Here are some general tips for setting rates:

1. Research your competition: Look at what similar services or products are being offered in

your market and what they charge. This will give you a baseline for what rates are acceptable.

2. Determine the value of your service or product: Consider the time and resources that go into producing or delivering your service or product. Also, consider the demand for your service or product, as well as any unique features or benefits it offers.

3. Consider your target market: Your target market will influence the rates you set. If your target market is price-sensitive, you may need to set lower rates to remain competitive.

4. Factor in your expenses: You need to make sure your rates cover your expenses, including the cost of materials, time, and overhead.

5. Test and adjust: It's important to test different rates and see how they perform. You may need to adjust your rates over time to ensure you're staying competitive and profitable.

It's important to note that setting rates is not an exact science and may require some trial and error to get right. It's also important to be transparent with your customers about your rates and why you've set them at a certain level.

BENEFIT OF SETTING YOUR RATES

As a freelancer or a service provider, setting your rates can offer several benefits:

1. Control over your income: When you set your rates, you have control over how much money you earn. You can set rates that are competitive yet profitable, taking into account your skills, experience, and the current market trends.

2. Attracting the right clients: When you set your rates, you can attract clients who value your work and are willing to pay what you're worth. This can help you establish long-term relationships with clients who appreciate the value you bring to the table.

3. Transparency and clarity: Setting your rates allows you to communicate clearly and transparently with your clients about how much you charge for your services. This can help avoid confusion or misunderstandings and build trust with your clients.

4. Building your brand: When you set your rates and deliver high-quality work, you can build a reputation as a skilled and reliable professional in your field. This can help you attract more clients and increase your earning potential over time.

5. Increased confidence: By setting your rates and communicating them confidently to clients, you can increase your own confidence in your skills and the value you bring to the table. This can lead to a more positive mindset and greater success in your business.

Chapter Three

CHAPTER THREE

CREATING AND SELLING DIGITAL PRODUCTS THAT WORKS

Creating and selling digital products is a business model where individuals or companies create digital products and sell them online. Digital products can include e-books, courses, software, music, graphics, and many others.

The process starts with identifying a market niche and creating a product that addresses the needs of that niche. Once the product is created, it needs to be marketed and promoted to the target audience. This can be done through social media, advertising, and other online channels.

Digital products are usually delivered electronically, which means that customers can access them immediately after purchase. Digital products are also easier to scale because they do not require physical inventory or shipping, and can be sold to customers anywhere in the world.

To sell digital products, individuals or companies can use online platforms such as Amazon, Etsy, and Shopify, or they can create their own website and online store. Digital products can be sold for a one-time fee or on a subscription basis, allowing for recurring revenue.

A business model that allows individuals or companies to create products that address the needs of a specific market niche and sell them online, delivering them electronically. It offers a scalable and flexible business model that can generate recurring revenue.

Creating and selling digital products has become an increasingly popular way to earn income online. Digital products are intangible goods that can be delivered electronically, such as e-books, courses, software, graphics, music, and more. Here are some steps to help you get started with creating and selling digital products:

1. Identify your niche: Choose a topic or subject that you are knowledgeable and passionate about. This will help you create high-quality content that your target audience will find valuable.

2. Research your market: Determine who your target audience is, what their pain points are, and what type of digital products they are most likely to buy.

3. Choose your product format: Decide on the type of digital product you want to create. This could be an e-book, video course, software, membership site, or any other format that suits your niche and audience.

4. Create your product: Use your expertise and knowledge to create high-quality content that provides value to your target audience.

5. Set your price: Research your market to determine the optimal price for your product. You may want to test different price points to see what works best for you.

6. Market your product: Use social media, email marketing, content marketing, and other strategies to promote your digital product to your target audience.

7. Deliver your product: Once a customer purchases your product, deliver it electronically. You can use a platform like Gumroad, SendOwl, or WooCommerce to handle the delivery process.

8. Customer support: Be available to provide customer support for your customers, such as answering questions or addressing issues with the product.

Remember that creating and selling digital products is a long-term game. It may take time to build a loyal following and generate consistent sales. However, if you create high-quality products that provide value to your target audience, you can build a successful digital product business over time.

TYPES OF DIGITAL PRODUCTS THAT WORKS

Digital products are intangible goods that are created and distributed electronically. They are products that can be downloaded or accessed online, and they include everything from software to ebooks, music, videos, online courses, and more. Here are some of the most popular types of digital products:

1. Software: This includes computer programs, mobile apps, and web applications. Software can be anything from a productivity tool to a game, and can be sold directly to consumers or through licensing agreements.

2. Ebooks: Digital books are becoming increasingly popular as people prefer to read on their electronic devices. Ebooks can be

purchased through online bookstores, such as Amazon's Kindle store.

3. Music: Digital music can be purchased through online music stores like iTunes, Amazon Music, and Spotify. It can also be streamed through services like Pandora and YouTube.

4. Videos: Digital videos can be anything from movies and TV shows to educational videos and short films. They can be purchased or rented through online video stores like iTunes, Amazon Video, and Google Play.

5. Online courses: These are educational programs that are delivered entirely online. They can be anything from language courses to software development courses and are often delivered through learning management systems like Udemy and Coursera.

6. Digital art: This includes everything from digital paintings to graphic designs and can be sold online through platforms like Etsy and Society6.

7. Website templates: Website templates are pre-designed website layouts that can be customized to fit the needs of the user. They can be purchased online through platforms like ThemeForest and Template Monster.

8. Stock photos: Stock photos are licensed images that can be used for commercial or personal use. They can be purchased through platforms like Shutterstock and iStock.

9. Digital subscriptions: These are recurring payments that give users access to exclusive content, services, or products. Examples include streaming services like Netflix and subscription boxes like Birchbox.

Overall, digital products are diverse and ever-evolving, making them a popular choice for businesses and consumers alike.

CREATING AND SELLING DIGITAL PRODUCTS ONLINE

Yes, that is correct. Creating and selling digital products is a popular way to make money online. With the increasing number of people using the internet, there is a growing demand for digital products such as ebooks, online courses, software, music, and digital art.

Digital products can be created by individuals, small businesses, or large corporations, and sold through various online platforms such as Amazon, Etsy, Udemy, and Shopify. Some people also create their own websites to sell their digital products directly to customers.

The advantage of selling digital products is that they can be created once and sold repeatedly, without the need for physical inventory or shipping. This allows for a high profit margin and scalability.

However, creating and selling digital products requires skills such as writing, design, programming, or video production, depending on the type of product. It also requires marketing skills to promote the product and reach the target audience.

THE BEST WAY IN CREATING AND SELLING DIGITAL PRODUCTS: ANOTHER POPULAR WAY TO MAKE MONEY ONLINE

Creating and selling digital products is a popular way to make money online. Here are some tips on how to create and sell digital products successfully:

1. Identify a market need: Before creating a digital product, it's essential to identify a market need. You can do this by conducting market research, asking for feedback from potential customers, or looking at what your competitors are doing.

2. Choose a profitable niche: Once you have identified a market need, you need to choose a

profitable niche. Look for niches that have high demand and low competition.

3. Create a valuable product: Your digital product should provide value to your customers. This could be in the form of information, tools, or entertainment. Ensure that your product is well-researched, well-written, and well-designed.

4. Use high-quality visuals: Visuals are crucial for digital products. Use high-quality images, graphics, and videos to make your product more attractive and engaging.

5. Use a user-friendly platform: Make sure your product is easy to use and navigate. This will help to reduce customer frustration and increase the chances of repeat purchases.

6. Use effective marketing strategies: Marketing is essential for selling digital products. Use social media, email marketing, SEO, and paid advertising to reach your target audience.

7. Provide excellent customer service: Providing excellent customer service is essential for

building customer loyalty and generating positive reviews. Be responsive to customer inquiries and complaints, and address any issues promptly.

By following these tips, you can create and sell digital products successfully and make money online.

THE BEST WAYS IN CREATING E-BOOKS, COURSES, AND SOFTWARE

Creating e-books, courses, and software can be a challenging process, but with the right tools and techniques, it can be an enjoyable and rewarding experience. Here are some of the best ways to create these types of digital products:

Creating E-books:

1. Choose a Topic: The first step in creating an e-book is to decide on a topic that you are knowledgeable and passionate about. Your topic

should be something that people are interested in and that you can provide unique insights into.

2. Research: Once you have decided on your topic, you need to research it thoroughly. This will involve reading books, articles, and online resources related to your topic. You can also interview experts in the field to get additional insights.

3. Outline Your Book: Once you have done your research, you need to outline your book. Your outline should include chapters, subheadings, and key points that you want to cover in each section.

4. Write Your Book: With your outline in place, you can start writing your book. It's important to write in a clear and concise manner and to provide examples and stories to illustrate your points.

5. Edit and Proofread: Once you have finished writing your book, you need to edit and proofread it. You can do this yourself, but it's

often helpful to hire a professional editor to ensure that your book is error-free and flows smoothly.

6. Format and Publish: Once your book is complete, you need to format it for e-book readers and publish it on platforms such as Amazon Kindle, Apple iBooks, and Barnes & Noble Nook.

Creating Courses:

1. Choose a Topic: The first step in creating a course is to choose a topic that you are knowledgeable and passionate about. Your topic should be something that people are interested in and that you can provide unique insights into.

2. Determine Your Learning Objectives: Once you have chosen your topic, you need to determine your learning objectives. These are the specific skills and knowledge that you want your students to gain from taking your course.

3. Create Your Curriculum: With your learning objectives in mind, you can start creating your curriculum. This will involve creating lessons, exercises, and assessments that will help your students achieve their learning objectives.

4. Develop Your Content: Once you have your curriculum in place, you can start developing your content. This can include videos, slideshows, and written materials.

5. Create Your Platform: With your content in place, you need to create a platform for your course. This can be a website, a learning management system, or a third-party platform such as Udemy or Skillshare.

6. Launch Your Course: Once your platform is ready, you can launch your course. You should promote it through social media, email marketing, and other channels to attract students.

Creating Software:

1. Choose Your Programming Language: The first step in creating software is to choose your programming language. This will depend on the type of software you are creating and your personal preferences.

2. Plan Your Software: Once you have chosen your programming language, you need to plan your software. This will involve creating a specification document that outlines the features and functionality of your software.

3. Develop Your Software: With your plan in place, you can start developing your software. This will involve coding, testing, and debugging your software to ensure that it works as intended.

4. Design Your User Interface: Once your software is functional, you need to design your user interface. This will involve creating a visual design that is intuitive and easy to use.

5. Test and Refine: Once your user interface is in place, you need to test your software and refine it based on user feedback. This will involve identifying bugs and usability issues and making adjustments to improve the user experience.

HOW TO MARKET ONLINE PRODUCT EFFECTIVELY

Marketing an online product effectively requires a well-thought-out plan and a combination of different strategies. Here are some steps that can help you market your online product effectively:

1. Identify your target audience: Before you start marketing your product, you need to know who your target audience is. Conduct market research to identify the demographics, interests, and needs of your target audience.

2. Develop a marketing strategy: Based on your target audience research, develop a marketing strategy that includes a mix of different marketing channels such as social media, email marketing, search engine optimization (SEO), paid advertising, influencer marketing, content marketing, and more.

3. Create a compelling website: Your website is the primary destination for your target audience,

so make sure it is visually appealing, easy to navigate, and showcases your product effectively.

4. Optimize for search engines: Use SEO techniques to optimize your website and product pages for search engines, which will help you rank higher in search results and drive more traffic to your website.

5. Leverage social media: Use social media platforms to promote your product, engage with your audience, and build brand awareness.

6. Email marketing: Use email marketing to stay in touch with your customers and prospects, promote your product, and provide value through newsletters and special offers.

7. Paid advertising: Consider using paid advertising channels such as Google Ads or Facebook Ads to drive more traffic and sales to your website.

8. Use influencer marketing: Partner with influencers in your industry who have a large

following and can help promote your product to their audience.

9. Provide excellent customer service: Provide excellent customer service to your customers, which will help you build trust and loyalty and lead to positive reviews and word-of-mouth marketing.

Overall, marketing an online product effectively requires a combination of different strategies, ongoing testing and optimization, and a deep understanding of your target audience.

Chapter Four

CHAPTER FOUR

AFFILIATE MARKETING

Affiliate marketing is a performance-based marketing strategy in which a company rewards affiliates for promoting their products or services. Essentially, affiliates are paid a commission for every sale or lead they generate for the company.

Affiliate marketing works by creating a partnership between the company and the affiliate. The company provides the affiliate with a unique tracking link or code, which the affiliate uses to promote the company's products or services. When a customer clicks on the affiliate's link and makes a purchase, the affiliate earns a commission.

One of the key benefits of affiliate marketing is that it allows companies to expand their reach and tap into new audiences without the need for significant upfront investment in advertising or marketing. Instead, they pay a commission only when a sale or lead is generated.

For affiliates, the benefits of affiliate marketing include the ability to earn passive income by promoting products or services they believe in, without the need to create their own products or handle customer service.

To be successful in affiliate marketing, both companies and affiliates need to choose the right products or services to promote, create high-quality content to promote those products or services, and build trust with their audiences. Companies need to provide affiliates with the necessary tools and resources to promote their products effectively, while affiliates need to focus on building a loyal following and delivering value to their audiences.

TYPES OF AFFILIATE MARKETING

There are several types of affiliate marketing, including:

1. Pay-per-click (PPC) affiliate marketing: This type of affiliate marketing involves affiliates earning commissions for every click made on their affiliate link, regardless of whether or not the click results in a sale.

2. Pay-per-lead (PPL) affiliate marketing: With PPL affiliate marketing, affiliates are paid for every lead or potential customer that they send to the merchant's website. This could include signing up for a newsletter, filling out a form, or requesting more information.

3. Pay-per-sale (PPS) affiliate marketing: In PPS affiliate marketing, affiliates earn a commission only when a sale is made through their unique affiliate link.

4. Two-tier affiliate marketing: This type of affiliate marketing allows affiliates to earn

commissions not only for their own sales, but also for the sales made by the affiliates they recruit to the program.

5. Multi-level marketing (MLM): MLM is similar to two-tier affiliate marketing, but it typically involves a more complex compensation structure in which affiliates earn commissions not only for their own sales and the sales of the affiliates they recruit, but also for the sales of the affiliates recruited by those affiliates, and so on. MLM is sometimes criticized for being a pyramid scheme.

6. Influencer marketing: Influencer marketing is a form of affiliate marketing that involves partnering with social media influencers to promote a product or service to their followers. Influencers may earn a commission for every sale made through their unique affiliate link.

EXPLORE HOW TO BECOME AN AFFILIATE MARKETER

Becoming an affiliate marketer involves several steps, including selecting a niche, choosing affiliate programs, building a website, creating content, and promoting your affiliate links. Here are some steps to follow:

1. Choose a niche: Decide on a specific area of interest for your affiliate marketing efforts. This can be anything from fitness to finance, beauty to technology, or any other topic you have a passion for.

2. Research affiliate programs: Look for affiliate programs that are relevant to your niche. There are numerous affiliate programs out there, and you can use platforms like ShareASale, Commission Junction, or Amazon Associates to find programs that fit your niche.

3. Join affiliate programs: After identifying affiliate programs that fit your niche, sign up for them. Most affiliate programs are free to join.

4. Build a website: Building a website is crucial to the success of your affiliate marketing efforts. You can use platforms like WordPress or Wix to create a website or hire a web designer to create one for you.

5. Create content: Create quality content that is relevant to your niche and incorporates your affiliate links. The content could include blog posts, product reviews, tutorials, or any other type of content that your audience finds useful.

6. Promote your content: Once you have created quality content, promote it through social media, email marketing, or other channels to drive traffic to your website and increase your chances of earning commissions through your affiliate links.

7. Track your progress: Monitor your affiliate marketing efforts and track your progress using

analytics tools. This will help you understand which strategies are working and which ones need improvement.

8. Keep learning: Stay up-to-date with the latest trends and best practices in affiliate marketing. Join affiliate marketing communities and attend conferences to network with other marketers and learn from industry experts.

In summary, becoming an affiliate marketer requires dedication, patience, and a willingness to learn. By following these steps, you can start your journey to becoming a successful affiliate marketer.

WHAT IS THE RIGHT MINDSET OF AN AFFILIATE MARKETER?

The right mindset for an affiliate marketer is one that is focused on providing value to their audience and building strong relationships with them. Here are some key elements of the right mindset for affiliate marketing:

1. A focus on the audience: Successful affiliate marketers prioritize the needs and interests of their audience. They are constantly thinking about what will be valuable to their audience and how they can provide it.

2. Patience and persistence: Affiliate marketing can take time to produce results, so it's important to have patience and persistence. It's essential to keep working hard, even if it takes a while to see results.

3. A commitment to learning: Affiliate marketing is constantly evolving, so it's important to stay up-to-date with the latest trends and strategies. Successful affiliate marketers are committed to learning and are always looking for ways to improve their skills and knowledge.

4. A focus on quality over quantity: It's better to have a smaller audience that is highly engaged and responsive than a large audience that is indifferent. Successful affiliate marketers prioritize quality over quantity.

5. Honesty and transparency: Trust is essential in affiliate marketing, and successful affiliate marketers are honest and transparent with their audience. They disclose their affiliate relationships and only promote products and services that they genuinely believe in.

Overall, the right mindset for affiliate marketing is one that is focused on providing value to the audience, building strong relationships, and staying committed to learning and improvement.

HOW TO CHOOSE THE RIGHT PRODUCTS TO PROMOTE

Choosing the right products to promote depends on a variety of factors, including your target audience, your niche, and the products themselves. Here are some steps you can follow to choose the right products to promote:

1. Determine your target audience: Who are you trying to reach with your promotions? What are their interests, needs, and preferences? Understanding your target audience will help you identify the products that will resonate with them.

2. Define your niche: What industry or topic are you promoting products in? Narrowing down your focus to a specific niche will help you identify the types of products that will be most relevant to your audience.

3. Research products: Once you know your audience and niche, start researching products that align with those parameters. Look for products that have a good reputation, are high quality, and are in demand.

4. Consider the commission rate: If you're promoting products as an affiliate marketer, be sure to consider the commission rate you'll earn on each sale. Look for products that offer a high commission rate, but also ensure that the

products are relevant and valuable to your audience.

5. Evaluate the competition: Take a look at what other marketers in your niche are promoting. Are there products that are consistently popular? Are there gaps in the market that you can fill with your promotions?

6. Test and track: Once you've identified products to promote, test them out to see how they perform with your audience. Use analytics tools to track your results and make adjustments as needed.

Overall, choosing the right products to promote takes time and research. By understanding your audience, niche, and competition, you'll be able to identify products that will resonate with your audience and help you achieve your marketing goals.

BASIC OBJECTIVE FOR THE RIGHT PRODUCTS TO PROMOTE

The objective of promoting the right products is to increase sales and revenue for a business. It is essential to select products that are likely to be in demand and appeal to the target audience. By promoting the right products, businesses can increase their customer base, build brand loyalty, and gain a competitive edge in the market.

The selection of the right products to promote depends on several factors, including the target market, the industry, and the overall marketing strategy of the business. For instance, a business that targets the millennial demographic may focus on promoting eco-friendly and sustainable products that align with this audience's values.

Promoting the right products also involves identifying the unique selling points of the products and highlighting them in marketing campaigns. This could involve showcasing the features, benefits, and value of the products through different channels, including social media, email marketing, and advertising.

Ultimately, the objective of promoting the right products is to drive sales, increase brand awareness, and foster customer loyalty. By identifying and promoting the products that are most likely to resonate with their target audience, businesses can achieve these objectives and ultimately succeed in the market.

HOW TO MAXIMIZE YOUR EARNINGS

There are several ways to maximize your earnings, including:

1. Invest in yourself: One of the best ways to maximize your earnings is to invest in yourself by developing new skills or enhancing your existing ones. This can make you more valuable to your current employer or help you find higher-paying job opportunities.

2. Negotiate your salary: When you are offered a job or a promotion, it's important to negotiate your salary to ensure you are being paid what you're worth. Do your research on average salaries for similar positions and be prepared to make a case for why you deserve more.

3. Start a side hustle: Starting a side hustle can help you earn extra income outside of your day job. Look for opportunities that align with your skills and interests, and be prepared to put in the time and effort required to make it successful.

4. Invest in the stock market: Investing in the stock market can be a good way to earn passive income over time. However, it's important to do your research and make informed decisions to minimize risk.

5. Live below your means: One of the simplest ways to maximize your earnings is to live below your means. This means avoiding unnecessary expenses and saving as much money as possible. The more you save, the more you can invest in your future earnings potential.

PRINCIPLES TO MAXIMIZE YOUR EARNINGS AS AN AFFILIATE MARKETERS

As an affiliate marketer, your goal is to maximize your earnings by promoting and selling products or services offered by other companies. Here are some principles that can help you achieve this:

1. Choose the right products: The first step in maximizing your earnings as an affiliate marketer is to choose the right products to promote. Select products that are in high demand, have a good reputation, and offer high commissions. Consider the target audience and their needs and preferences when making your selection.

2. Build a loyal audience: Building a loyal audience is essential to the success of your affiliate marketing efforts. Provide valuable content and build trust with your audience by being honest, transparent, and authentic. Engage with your audience through social media, email

marketing, and other channels to build a strong relationship.

3. Use multiple channels: Use multiple channels to reach your audience and promote your affiliate products. This can include your website or blog, social media, email marketing, video marketing, and paid advertising. By using multiple channels, you can reach a wider audience and increase your chances of making sales.

4. Test and optimize: Test different strategies and tactics to see what works best for your audience and your niche. Use analytics and tracking tools to measure your results and optimize your campaigns for maximum earnings.

5. Stay up-to-date: Stay up-to-date with the latest trends and developments in your niche and the affiliate marketing industry. Attend conferences, join forums, and follow industry leaders and influencers to stay informed and gain insights that can help you improve your earnings.

By following these principles, you can maximize your earnings as an affiliate marketer and build a successful and profitable business.

☞ Chapter Five ☙

CHAPTER FIVE

E-COMMERCE

E-commerce, short for electronic commerce, refers to the buying and selling of goods and services online through the internet. This involves a range of activities including online shopping, online banking, online ticket booking, and online auctions. E-commerce has become increasingly popular in recent years due to the convenience and flexibility it offers to consumers and businesses.

E-commerce typically involves a website or online platform where customers can browse and purchase products or services, and where businesses can manage their sales, inventory, and customer relationships. Payment and delivery methods vary depending on the specific e-commerce platform and the products or services being sold.

E-commerce has had a significant impact on the global economy, enabling businesses to reach a wider audience and consumers to access a greater variety of products and services. However, it has also raised concerns around security and privacy, as well as the impact on traditional brick-and-mortar businesses.

TYPES OF E-COMMERCE

There are several types of e-commerce, including:

1. Business-to-Consumer (B2C) e-commerce: This is the most common type of e-commerce, in which businesses sell products or services directly to individual consumers through an online platform or website.

2. Business-to-Business (B2B) e-commerce: This type of e-commerce involves transactions between businesses, such as manufacturers and wholesalers selling products to retailers or other businesses.

3. Consumer-to-Consumer (C2C) e-commerce: In this type of e-commerce, consumers sell products or services to other consumers through online platforms, such as eBay or Craigslist.

4. Consumer-to-Business (C2B) e-commerce: This type of e-commerce involves individual consumers selling products or services to

businesses, such as freelance designers or consultants.

5. Business-to-Government (B2G) e-commerce: This type of e-commerce involves transactions between businesses and government entities, such as government procurement of goods and services.

6. Government-to-Consumer (G2C) e-commerce: In this type of e-commerce, government agencies sell products or services directly to individual consumers through online platforms or websites, such as issuing licenses or permits.

7. Mobile commerce (m-commerce): This type of e-commerce involves transactions conducted through mobile devices, such as smartphones or tablets.

8. Social commerce: This type of e-commerce involves buying and selling products or services through social media platforms, such as Facebook, Instagram, or Pinterest.

IMPORTANCE AND BENEFIT OF E-COMMERCE

E-commerce, or electronic commerce, refers to the buying and selling of goods and services over the internet. In recent years, e-commerce has become an increasingly important part of the global economy, and its importance and benefits are numerous.

1. Increased convenience: E-commerce provides consumers with the convenience of shopping from the comfort of their own homes or anywhere with an internet connection. This eliminates the need for physical travel to a brick-and-mortar store, saving time and effort.

2. Global reach: E-commerce allows businesses to reach a global customer base, breaking down geographical barriers and expanding their market. This can lead to increased sales and revenue.

3. Lower costs: E-commerce businesses can operate with lower overhead costs, as they do

not need to maintain a physical storefront or hire as many staff. This can translate to lower prices for consumers and increased profitability for businesses.

4. Personalization: E-commerce businesses can use data analytics to personalize the shopping experience for each customer, offering product recommendations and promotions tailored to their individual preferences and buying history.

5. Increased competition: E-commerce has increased competition among businesses, leading to a more diverse and competitive marketplace. This can benefit consumers through lower prices and better quality products.

6. Improved inventory management: E-commerce businesses can more easily manage their inventory and avoid overstocking or understocking products. This can lead to more efficient operations and increased profitability.

7. Access to niche markets: E-commerce businesses can reach niche markets that may be

too small or dispersed for traditional brick-and-mortar stores to target. This can open up new opportunities for businesses and provide consumers with access to unique products and services.

In summary, the importance and benefits of e-commerce are vast and varied. From increased convenience and global reach to lower costs and improved personalization, e-commerce has transformed the way we shop and do business.

SETTING UP AN ONLINE STORE

Setting up an online store can seem daunting, but with the right tools and guidance, it can be a relatively simple process. Here are some steps to consider when setting up your online store:

1. Choose your platform: There are several e-commerce platforms to choose from, such as Shopify, WooCommerce, Magento, and more.

Consider the features each platform offers, their pricing, and the level of customization they allow.

2. Select a domain name and hosting: Choose a domain name that is easy to remember and reflects your brand. You will also need to select a hosting provider that can handle your website traffic and support your online store.

3. Design your store: Your online store's design should reflect your brand and be visually appealing to your customers. Consider hiring a web designer or using pre-designed templates to help you create a professional-looking store.

4. Add your products: Upload your product images, descriptions, and prices to your online store. Organize your products into categories and add any necessary tags to make them easy to find.

5. Set up payment options: Your customers will need a way to pay for their purchases. Consider

using a payment gateway, such as PayPal or Stripe, to securely process payments.

6. Choose shipping and delivery options: Decide how you will ship your products to customers and calculate shipping costs based on weight and destination. Consider offering different shipping options, such as standard or expedited, to give your customers more flexibility.

7. Test your website: Before launching your online store, make sure everything is working correctly by testing your website's functionality, links, and payment processing.

8. Launch your store: Once everything is ready, it's time to launch your online store. Share your store's URL on your social media channels, email list, and other marketing channels to drive traffic to your site.

Remember, setting up an online store takes time and effort, but with the right tools and strategies, you can create a successful e-commerce business.

BEST METHOD OF SETTING UP AN ONLINE STORE

There are several methods for setting up an online store, and the best method depends on your specific needs and requirements. However, here are some general steps you can follow:

1. Choose an eCommerce platform: There are many eCommerce platforms available, such as Shopify, WooCommerce, Magento, and BigCommerce. Choose a platform that best fits your needs, budget, and technical skills.

2. Register a domain name: Your domain name is the address of your online store. Choose a name that is easy to remember, relevant to your business, and available for registration.

3. Choose a web hosting provider: A web hosting provider stores your website's files and makes them available online. Choose a reliable and affordable hosting provider that offers excellent uptime, customer support, and security features.

4. Design your online store: Choose a professional and attractive theme for your online store. Customize it to fit your brand and products. Make sure your store is easy to navigate, responsive, and optimized for search engines.

5. Set up payment gateways: Choose a payment gateway that supports your preferred payment methods, such as credit cards, PayPal, or Apple Pay. Make sure your payment gateway is secure and compliant with relevant regulations.

6. Add products: Add products to your online store, including product descriptions, images, prices, and inventory levels.

7. Set up shipping options: Choose shipping carriers and methods that best fit your products and customers' needs. Set up shipping rates and rules.

8. Launch your online store: Test your online store thoroughly before launching it. Make sure all features and functionalities work correctly.

Promote your online store through social media, email marketing, and other channels.

Remember to monitor your online store's performance regularly, optimize it for better results, and respond to customer feedback and complaints promptly.

TYPE OF ONLINE STORE TO SET UP

Deciding on the type of online store to set up depends on several factors such as your interests, skills, target audience, and market demand. Here are some ideas for different types of online stores that you could consider:

1. Niche product store: Focus on selling a specific type of product, such as sustainable fashion, eco-friendly products, pet supplies, or unique handmade items.

2. Dropshipping store: Create an online store that offers products from third-party suppliers without keeping any inventory.

3. Digital products store: Sell digital products such as e-books, online courses, music, or software.

4. Subscription-based store: Offer a subscription service for products such as meal kits, beauty boxes, or fitness products.

5. Marketplace store: Create an online marketplace where multiple vendors can sell their products.

6. Service-based store: Offer services such as web design, content writing, or consulting.

7. Print-on-demand store: Create custom-designed products such as t-shirts, mugs, or phone cases, and print them on demand.

Ultimately, the best type of online store for you to set up will depend on your interests, skills, and the needs of your target audience. Conduct market research and consider your personal strengths to find the right fit for your business.

CHOOSING A NICHE

Choosing a niche involves identifying a specific area or market that you want to specialize in and targeting your efforts towards that particular group of customers. Here are some steps to help you choose a niche:

1. Identify your interests: Start by making a list of topics that you are interested in or passionate about. This could be anything from cooking to fitness to technology.

2. Research potential niches: Once you have identified your interests, research potential niches within those areas. Look for gaps in the market or areas where there is high demand but not enough supply.

3. Consider your skills and expertise: Think about your skills and expertise and how they can be applied to your chosen niche. For example, if you have a background in marketing, you may

be able to specialize in helping small businesses with their marketing efforts.

4. Evaluate the competition: Look at the competition within your chosen niche and evaluate their strengths and weaknesses. This will help you identify areas where you can differentiate yourself and offer something unique.

5. Test your idea: Before committing to a niche, test your idea by talking to potential customers and getting feedback on your product or service. This will help you refine your offering and ensure that there is demand for what you are offering.

Remember that choosing a niche is an iterative process and may require some trial and error. Don't be afraid to pivot if your initial idea isn't working out. With persistence and dedication, you can build a successful business in a niche that you love.

IMPORTANCE OF CHOOSING THE RIGHT NICHE

Choosing the right niche is crucial for any individual or business looking to establish themselves in a particular market. Here are some reasons why:

1. Targeted Audience: By choosing a niche, you can better understand your target audience, their interests, and their needs. This allows you to create products or services that cater to their specific requirements, making your offering more appealing to them.

2. Competition: Niche markets are generally less competitive than broader markets, which makes it easier for you to establish yourself as a leader in that space. This can help you gain a competitive advantage, which is critical to long-term success.

3. Branding: Choosing a niche helps you to establish a clear brand identity. When you focus on a particular market, you can develop a unique

value proposition that sets you apart from your competitors.

4. Expertise: By specializing in a particular niche, you can become an expert in that area. This can help you to build credibility with your customers, which is essential for building trust and long-term relationships.

5. Cost-effective marketing: By targeting a specific audience, you can save on marketing costs. Instead of trying to reach a broad audience, you can focus your marketing efforts on the people who are most likely to be interested in your product or service.

Overall, choosing the right niche is critical to the success of any business or individual. It allows you to focus on a specific audience, differentiate yourself from competitors, establish credibility, and save on marketing costs.

IMPLICATION OF CHOOSING THE WRONG NICHE

Choosing the wrong niche can have significant implications for your business or project. Here are a few potential consequences:

1. Limited audience: If you choose a niche that is too narrow or doesn't have a significant audience, you may struggle to attract and retain customers or followers. This can limit your growth potential and make it difficult to build a sustainable business.

2. Lack of passion: If you choose a niche solely for its profitability or market demand, but don't have a genuine interest or passion for it, you may quickly become burnt out or lose motivation. This can negatively impact your productivity and creativity, and ultimately harm your business.

3. Increased competition: Choosing a popular or trendy niche may seem like a good idea, but it

can also mean that you'll face a lot of competition from other businesses or individuals. This can make it more challenging to stand out and make a name for yourself, and can also drive down prices and profits.

4. Difficulty in monetizing: If you choose a niche that doesn't have a clear path to monetization, you may struggle to generate revenue or turn a profit. This can make it challenging to sustain your business over the long term.

5. Poor customer fit: If your niche doesn't align with your target audience's needs, interests, or values, you may struggle to build a loyal customer base or develop meaningful relationships with your followers. This can harm your reputation and make it more challenging to grow your business over time.

In summary, choosing the wrong niche can have significant implications for your business or project, including limited audience, lack of passion, increased competition, difficulty in monetizing, and poor customer fit. It's essential to carefully consider your options and choose a niche that aligns with your goals, strengths, and interests, as well as the needs and preferences of your target audience.

DRIVING TRAFFIC TO YOUR SITE

Driving traffic to a website involves various strategies and tactics that can be used to increase the number of visitors to the site. Here are some effective ways to drive traffic to your website:

1. Search Engine Optimization (SEO): SEO is the practice of optimizing your website's content and structure to rank higher in search engine results. This can help improve visibility and attract more organic traffic to your site.

2. Social Media Marketing: Social media is a powerful tool for driving traffic to your site. By creating engaging content and promoting it on social media platforms such as Facebook,

Twitter, LinkedIn, and Instagram, you can attract visitors to your site.

3. Email Marketing: Email marketing involves sending promotional emails to your subscribers or customers. This can be an effective way to drive traffic to your site, especially if you have a large email list.

4. Content Marketing: Creating valuable and engaging content that appeals to your target audience can help drive traffic to your site. This can include blog posts, videos, infographics, and other types of content.

5. Paid Advertising: Paid advertising can be an effective way to drive traffic to your site, especially if you're looking for quick results. This can include Google Ads, social media ads, display ads, and other forms of online advertising.

Overall, the key to driving traffic to your site is to focus on creating high-quality content that appeals to your target audience and promoting it through various channels. By using a combination of these tactics, you can attract more visitors to your site and ultimately increase your conversions and revenue.

IMPORTANCE OF DRIVING TRAFFIC TO YOUR SITE

Driving traffic to your site is critical for several reasons:

1. Increased Visibility: When you drive traffic to your site, more people become aware of your brand, product, or service. This can lead to increased visibility and awareness, which can be essential for building a strong online presence.

2. Higher Conversion Rates: The more traffic you have on your site, the greater the chances of converting visitors into customers. By driving traffic to your site, you increase your chances of generating leads and making sales.

3. Improved SEO: Search engines consider traffic volume when ranking sites, so driving traffic to your site can improve your search engine optimization (SEO). The more traffic you have, the higher your site will rank in search engine results pages (SERPs).

4. Increased Revenue: More traffic can lead to more sales, which can result in increased revenue. If you have an e-commerce site, driving traffic to your site can be critical for generating revenue.

5. Better Analytics: By driving traffic to your site, you can gain a better understanding of your audience and their behavior. You can track user engagement and analyze data to make informed decisions about your site's content, design, and marketing strategy.

Overall, driving traffic to your site is critical for building a successful online presence, generating leads and sales, and increasing revenue.

Chapter Six

CHAPTER SIX

ONLINE ADVERTISING

Online advertising refers to any form of marketing communication that is delivered via the internet to promote a product or service. It is a way for businesses to reach their target audience and drive traffic to their website or online store.

There are many different types of online advertising, including display ads, search engine ads, social media ads, video ads, and email marketing. Each type of advertising has its own benefits and can be effective in reaching different audiences.

One of the advantages of online advertising is its ability to target specific audiences based on factors such as location, demographics, interests, and online behavior. This allows businesses to reach the people who are most likely to be interested in their products or services, and can result in a higher return on investment (ROI).

Online advertising can also be more cost-effective than traditional advertising methods, as it often allows businesses to pay only when someone clicks on their ad or takes a desired action on their website.

However, online advertising can also be competitive, and businesses need to have a strong understanding of their target audience and the best platforms and strategies for reaching them in order to be successful.

DIFFERENT TYPES OF ONLINE ADVERTISING AND IT IMPORTANCE

There are several types of online advertising, including:

1. **Display Advertising:** This type of advertising involves placing banner ads on websites, typically in the form of images or videos.

2. **Search Engine Advertising:** This type of advertising involves placing ads on search engine result pages, typically in the form of text ads.

3. **Social Media Advertising:** This type of advertising involves promoting products or services through social media platforms such as Facebook, Instagram, and Twitter.

4. **Video Advertising:** This type of advertising involves placing ads in online videos, typically in the form of pre-roll ads that play before the video starts.

5. **Native Advertising:** This type of advertising involves promoting products or services through sponsored content that appears in the same format as the website or platform on which it is displayed.

Online advertising is important for several reasons:

1. **Increased reach:** With the growth of the internet, online advertising allows businesses to reach a much larger audience than traditional forms of advertising.

2. **Targeted advertising:** Online advertising allows businesses to target specific audiences based on demographics, interests, and behaviors.

3. **Measurable results:** Online advertising allows businesses to track and measure the effectiveness of their campaigns in real-time, providing valuable insights into consumer behavior and preferences.

4. **Cost-effective:** Online advertising can be more cost-effective than traditional forms of advertising, as businesses can set budgets and only pay for clicks or impressions.

5. **Brand building**: Online advertising can help businesses build their brand and increase brand awareness among consumers.

PAY-PER-CLICK (PPC) ADVERTISING

Pay-per-click (PPC) advertising is a type of online advertising in which advertisers pay each time a user clicks on one of their ads. PPC ads are typically displayed on search engine results pages (SERPs), social media platforms, and other websites, and are often targeted to specific keywords or audiences.

PPC advertising is often used as part of a larger digital marketing strategy, and can be an effective way to drive traffic and sales to a website. Some of the benefits of PPC advertising include:

1. Highly targeted advertising: Advertisers can target specific keywords, demographics, and geographic locations to ensure their ads are seen by the right people.

2. Measurable results: PPC advertising platforms provide detailed analytics and tracking tools that allow advertisers to measure the success of their campaigns and make data-driven decisions.

3. Cost control: Advertisers only pay when someone clicks on their ads, so they can control their advertising costs and adjust their budget as needed.

4. Fast results: PPC campaigns can be launched quickly and can start generating results immediately.

However, there are also some potential drawbacks to PPC advertising, including:

1. Cost: While advertisers can control their budget, the cost per click can be high for certain keywords and industries.

2. Click fraud: Some individuals or bots may intentionally click on ads to drive up costs for advertisers.

3. Competition: As more advertisers enter the PPC space, competition for keywords and ad space can increase, driving up costs and making it harder to stand out.

Overall, PPC advertising can be an effective way to drive traffic and sales to a website, but it's important for advertisers to carefully plan and execute their campaigns to maximize their return on investment.

BENEFIT OF PAY-PER-CLICK (PPC) ADVERTISING

Pay-per-click (PPC) advertising offers several benefits for businesses, including:

1. Targeted Advertising: PPC ads allow businesses to target specific demographics, geographic locations, interests, and behavior patterns. This

helps to ensure that ads are shown to the right audience, increasing the chances of conversion.

2. Measurable Results: PPC advertising platforms, such as Google Ads, provide detailed reports that show how many people clicked on the ad, how many conversions resulted from the ad, and how much was spent on the ad. This allows businesses to track their return on investment (ROI) and adjust their advertising strategies accordingly.

3. Cost-Effective: With PPC advertising, businesses only pay when someone clicks on their ad, which means they don't waste money on ad impressions that don't result in clicks or conversions. This can make PPC advertising more cost-effective than traditional advertising methods, such as print or TV ads.

4. Flexibility: PPC advertising allows businesses to set their own budgets and bids, and to make changes to their ads at any time. This flexibility allows businesses to adjust their advertising

strategies quickly in response to changes in the market or to the performance of their ads.

5. Immediate Results: Unlike other advertising methods that may take time to yield results, PPC advertising can generate immediate traffic and conversions to a website or landing page. This makes it an effective option for businesses looking to increase their online visibility and generate leads quickly.

SOCIAL MEDIA ADVERTISING

Social media advertising is a form of online advertising that uses social media platforms to reach and engage with target audiences. Social media advertising can take many different forms, including sponsored posts, display ads, video ads, and more.

The major social media platforms, such as Facebook, Instagram, Twitter, LinkedIn, and TikTok, offer various advertising options that allow businesses to reach their target audience in different ways. For example, Facebook offers sponsored posts that appear in users' newsfeeds, Instagram offers sponsored stories and posts, and LinkedIn offers sponsored content and ads.

Social media advertising offers many benefits to businesses, including the ability to target specific audiences based on their interests, demographics, and behavior. It can also help businesses reach a wider audience than traditional advertising methods, as social media platforms have millions of active users.

However, social media advertising can also be challenging, as competition for ad space can be intense, and businesses need to ensure that their ads are engaging and relevant to their target audience. Additionally, social media platforms are constantly changing their algorithms and ad policies, so businesses need to stay up-to-date on these changes to ensure their ads are effective.

Overall, social media advertising can be a powerful tool for businesses looking to reach and engage with their target audience online.

BENEFIT OF SOCIAL MEDIA ADVERTISING AND HOW TO DRIVE TRAFFIC

Social media advertising can be beneficial for businesses in a variety of ways, including:

1. Targeted Advertising: Social media platforms have sophisticated targeting options that allow businesses to reach their ideal audience based on factors such as age, gender, location, interests, and behavior.

2. Cost-Effective: Social media advertising can be cost-effective compared to traditional advertising methods. It allows businesses to set a budget and pay only when someone clicks on their ad or takes a specific action.

3. Increased Brand Awareness: Social media advertising can help businesses increase their brand awareness by reaching a large audience and exposing them to their products or services.

4. Driving Traffic: Social media advertising can drive traffic to a business's website or landing page, which can lead to increased sales and conversions.

To drive traffic through social media advertising, businesses can consider the following tips:

1. Choose the Right Platform: Businesses should choose the social media platforms that their target audience is most active on to ensure maximum reach.

2. Use Eye-Catching Visuals: Visuals are essential in social media advertising as they can grab the audience's attention and increase engagement. Use high-quality images and videos that reflect the brand and its message.

3. Create Compelling Ad Copy: The ad copy should be engaging and compelling enough to entice the audience to click on the ad and visit the business's website or landing page.

4. Use Call-to-Actions (CTAs): CTAs are essential in social media advertising as they encourage the audience to take action. Use CTAs that are clear, concise, and aligned with the business's objective.

5. Monitor and Adjust: Businesses should continuously monitor their social media ad campaigns to see what is working and what isn't.

They can then adjust their strategies accordingly to ensure maximum ROI.

EFFECTIVE ADS

Effective ads are those that successfully capture the attention of their target audience, communicate a clear message, and ultimately lead to a desired action or response. Here are some key elements that can make ads more effective:

1. Audience targeting: Ads need to be targeted to the right audience to be effective. This means understanding who your ideal customer is and tailoring your message and creative to appeal to them.

2. Clear message: Ads should have a clear and concise message that is easy to understand. Avoid using jargon or complicated language that may confuse your audience.

3. Strong visuals: Visuals are often the first thing that catches people's attention. Use high-quality

images or videos that are relevant to your message and will capture the attention of your audience.

4. Call to action: Every ad should have a clear call to action that tells the audience what you want them to do next. This could be anything from clicking a link to making a purchase.

5. Emotional appeal: Ads that evoke strong emotions are often more effective. Consider using humor, nostalgia, or other emotions that will resonate with your audience.

6. Consistency: Consistency is key when it comes to branding and messaging. Make sure your ads are consistent with your brand's visual identity and messaging across all channels.

7. Test and optimize: Test different versions of your ads to see which ones perform best. This will help you optimize your ads and improve their effectiveness over time.

HOW TO CREATE EFFECTIVE ADS

Creating effective ads requires careful planning, strategic thinking, and an understanding of your target audience. Here are some tips that can help you create effective ads:

1. Know your target audience: Before you start creating ads, you need to have a clear understanding of your target audience. Who are they, what are their interests, and what motivates them? Once you have a clear picture of your audience, you can tailor your ads to appeal to their needs and preferences.

2. Define your unique selling proposition: Your unique selling proposition (USP) is what sets you apart from your competitors. It should be a clear and concise statement that highlights the benefits of your product or service. Your USP should be prominently featured in your ads.

3. Use attention-grabbing headlines: Your ad headline is the first thing people will see, so it

needs to be attention-grabbing. Use a clear, concise headline that communicates the value of your product or service.

4. Focus on benefits, not features: Your ads should focus on the benefits of your product or service, not just the features. People want to know how your product or service will improve their lives, not just what it does.

5. Use high-quality visuals: Visuals are a powerful tool in advertising. Use high-quality images or videos that are relevant to your product or service and appeal to your target audience.

6. Include a call-to-action: Your ads should always include a call-to-action (CTA) that tells people what you want them to do next. This could be anything from "Shop now" to "Learn more."

7. Test and optimize: Finally, it's important to test and optimize your ads to ensure they are effective. Test different headlines, visuals, and CTAs to see what works best, and use the data to optimize your ads for maximum impact.

By following these tips, you can create effective ads that capture the attention of your target audience and drive results for your business.

☞ Chapter Seven

CHAPTER SEVEN

SOCIAL MEDIA MARKETING

Social media marketing refers to the use of social media platforms, such as Facebook, Twitter, Instagram, LinkedIn, and others, to promote a product, service, or brand. This type of marketing involves creating and sharing content, as well as engaging with users and followers on social media platforms in order to build relationships and drive traffic to a website or other online presence.

Social media marketing can be an effective way to reach a large audience quickly and easily, as social media platforms have millions of users. It can also be a cost-effective way to promote a product or service, as many social media platforms offer free or low-cost options for businesses to create and share content.

Some common social media marketing strategies include creating engaging content, running paid social media ads, influencer marketing, and using social media analytics to track and optimize campaign performance. It's important for businesses to develop a social media marketing plan that aligns with their overall marketing and business goals, and to regularly monitor and adapt their social media strategies based on performance metrics and user feedback

HISTORY OF STRONG SOCIAL MEDIA PRESENCE TO BUSINESS

The rise of social media has had a significant impact on businesses in recent years. A strong social media presence can help businesses reach and engage with their target audience, increase brand awareness and recognition, and drive traffic to their website. Here is brief histories of how social media has transformed the way businesses interact with their customers:

1. The early years: In the early days of social media, businesses mainly used it as a way to promote their products and services. They would post updates about new products or sales and hope that people would see and share their posts. However, social media platforms were still relatively new, and businesses were still figuring out how to use them effectively.

2. The rise of Facebook: Facebook became the dominant social media platform in the mid-2000s, and businesses quickly realized its

potential as a marketing tool. They began creating Facebook pages and using them to interact with customers, share content, and run promotions. Facebook also introduced targeted advertising, which allowed businesses to reach specific demographics based on interests, location, and other factors.

3. The emergence of Twitter: Twitter emerged as another popular social media platform in the late 2000s, and businesses quickly began using it to share news, updates, and promotions. Twitter's real-time nature also made it a useful tool for customer service, as businesses could quickly respond to customer inquiries and complaints.

4. The rise of visual content: With the rise of Instagram and Pinterest in the early 2010s, businesses began to focus more on visual content. They started sharing photos and videos of their products, behind-the-scenes looks at their operations, and user-generated content.

This helped to humanize businesses and create a more personal connection with customers.

5. The importance of engagement: As social media platforms became more crowded, businesses realized that simply posting updates was not enough. They needed to actively engage with their audience and build relationships with customers. This meant responding to comments, asking for feedback, and creating content that encouraged interaction.

6. The era of influencer marketing: In recent years, influencer marketing has emerged as a popular strategy for businesses looking to reach new audiences. Influencers are individuals with a large following on social media who can promote products and services to their followers. This has become an effective way for businesses to reach niche audiences and create authentic connections with customers.

Overall, a strong social media presence has become essential for businesses of all sizes in the modern era. By leveraging the power of social media platforms, businesses can build brand awareness, engage with customers, and drive sales in ways that were not possible in the past.

BENEFIT OF SOCIAL MEDIA MARKETING

Social media marketing can bring numerous benefits to businesses, including:

1. Increased brand awareness: Social media platforms provide an excellent opportunity for businesses to increase their visibility and reach a larger audience.

2. Improved customer engagement: Social media allows businesses to interact with customers and respond to their questions, comments, and concerns in real-time.

3. Enhanced customer loyalty: By engaging with customers and providing them with valuable content, businesses can build a stronger relationship with their audience and encourage brand loyalty.

4. Increased website traffic: Social media platforms can drive traffic to a business's website, helping to improve search engine rankings and increase overall website traffic.

5. Cost-effective marketing: Compared to traditional forms of advertising, social media marketing can be more cost-effective, allowing businesses to reach a larger audience with a smaller budget.
6. Targeted advertising: Social media platforms provide powerful targeting options, allowing businesses to target specific audiences based on demographics, interests, and behaviors.
7. Access to valuable insights: Social media platforms provide businesses with valuable insights into their audience, including demographics, interests, and behaviors, which can help inform marketing and business strategies.

Overall, social media marketing can be a highly effective way for businesses to reach and engage with their audience, build brand awareness, and drive website traffic, all while being cost-effective and providing valuable insights into customer behavior.

IMPLICATION OF SOCIAL MEDIA MARKETING

Social media marketing refers to the use of social media platforms to promote a product, service, or brand. It has become an increasingly popular and effective marketing strategy, with businesses of all sizes using social media to reach and engage with their target audience. Here are some of the implications of social media marketing:

1. Increased reach: Social media marketing allows businesses to reach a wider audience than traditional marketing methods. By using social media platforms such as Facebook, Instagram, Twitter, and LinkedIn, businesses can reach millions of users with just a single post.

2. Improved brand awareness: Social media marketing can help businesses improve their brand awareness by creating engaging and shareable content that promotes their products

or services. This can lead to increased brand recognition and customer loyalty.

3. Enhanced customer engagement: Social media marketing allows businesses to engage with their customers in real-time. They can respond to customer queries, complaints, and feedback, which helps build trust and loyalty.

4. Cost-effective: Social media marketing can be a cost-effective way to promote a business. It is often less expensive than traditional marketing methods, such as print and television advertising.

5. Targeted advertising: Social media platforms allow businesses to target their advertising to specific audiences based on demographics, interests, and behaviors. This ensures that their advertising is more effective and reaches the right people.

6. Increased website traffic: Social media marketing can drive traffic to a business's

website, which can lead to increased sales and revenue.

7. Improved search engine rankings: Social media signals, such as likes, shares, and comments, can help improve a business's search engine rankings. This can lead to increased visibility and more website traffic.

Overall, social media marketing has many benefits for businesses, including increased reach, improved brand awareness, enhanced customer engagement, cost-effectiveness, targeted advertising, increased website traffic, and improved search engine rankings.

BUILDING A STRONG SOCIAL MEDIA PRESENCE

Building a strong social media presence takes time and effort, but it can be very beneficial for businesses, individuals, and organizations looking to grow their brand or reach a wider audience. Here are some tips to help you build a strong social media presence:

1. Define your brand: Before you start building a social media presence, it's important to define your brand and the message you want to convey to your audience. Determine your target audience and what type of content will resonate with them.

2. Choose the right platforms: Not all social media platforms are created equal. Choose the platforms that are most relevant to your target audience and where you can create the most impact. For example, LinkedIn is great for professional networking and B2B marketing, while Instagram is more visual and ideal for targeting a younger demographic.

3. Create engaging content: Your content is what will attract and engage your audience. Create high-quality, visually appealing content that is relevant to your audience and aligns with your brand message.

4. Be consistent: Consistency is key when it comes to building a social media presence. Post

regularly, engage with your audience, and respond to comments and messages in a timely manner.

5. Use hashtags: Hashtags can help your content get discovered by new audiences. Use relevant hashtags in your posts to increase visibility.

6. Leverage user-generated content: Encourage your followers to create content related to your brand and share it on social media. This can help increase engagement and build a sense of community around your brand.

7. Analyze your results: Track your social media metrics and adjust your strategy as needed. Use analytics tools to determine which types of content perform best and adjust your strategy accordingly.

By following these tips, you can build a strong social media presence and increase your reach and engagement with your target audience.

WHY IS BUILDING A STRONG SOCIAL MEDIA PRESENCE IMPORTANCE TO YOUR BUSINESS

Building a strong social media presence is essential to any business for several reasons:

1. Increased brand awareness: Social media provides an excellent platform to increase your brand's visibility and awareness among potential customers. By regularly posting high-quality content and engaging with your followers, you can establish your brand as an authority in your industry and build a strong online reputation.

2. Improved customer engagement: Social media allows you to interact with your customers in real-time, which can help you better understand their needs and preferences. By responding to their comments and messages, you can build strong relationships with your customers and improve their overall experience with your brand.

3. Cost-effective marketing: Compared to traditional marketing methods, social media marketing is relatively inexpensive. It allows small businesses to reach a large audience without breaking the bank, making it an excellent option for those with limited marketing budgets.

4. Increased website traffic: By sharing links to your website on your social media platforms, you can drive more traffic to your site and potentially increase your sales.

5. Competitive advantage: With so many businesses competing for attention online, having a strong social media presence can give you a competitive advantage. By standing out from the crowd with engaging content and exceptional customer service, you can attract more customers and grow your business.

CREATING ENGAGING CONTENT

Creating engaging content can be challenging, but there are several tips and strategies that you can use to make your content more interesting and appealing to your audience. Here are some ideas:

1. Know your audience: Understanding your audience and what they're interested in is crucial to creating content that resonates with them. Research their demographics, interests, and needs to tailor your content to their preferences.

2. Use storytelling: People love stories, and using storytelling in your content can help you connect with your audience on a deeper level. Use anecdotes, examples, and personal experiences to make your content more relatable and engaging.

3. Be informative: Providing useful and informative content is essential to building trust and authority with your audience. Offer insights,

tips, and practical advice that your audience can use in their daily lives.

4. Use visual aids: Incorporating images, videos, infographics, and other visual aids can make your content more visually appealing and engaging. Visuals can also help you convey complex information more effectively.

5. Keep it concise: Attention spans are short, and people are busy. Make sure your content is concise and to the point. Use short paragraphs, bullet points, and subheadings to break up long blocks of text.

6. Add interactivity: Interactive content, such as quizzes, surveys, and polls, can help increase engagement and make your content more fun and memorable.

7. Use humor: Humor can help you connect with your audience and make your content more entertaining. Use humor where appropriate, but be careful not to overdo it or use inappropriate humor.

Remember, creating engaging content takes time, effort, and practice. Keep experimenting with different strategies and techniques until you find what works best for your audience.

HOW TO CREATE ENGAGING CONTENT TOWARD ACHIEVING HIGH-END RESULT

Creating engaging content is a key factor in achieving high-end results. Here are some tips to help you create engaging content:

1. Know your audience: Before creating any content, it is essential to know your audience. Determine their interests, needs, and pain points. This will help you create content that resonates with them.

2. Choose the right format: Different formats of content resonate with different audiences. Depending on your audience and the message you want to convey, choose the right format,

such as videos, blogs, infographics, podcasts, or social media posts.

3. Use a compelling headline: Your headline should grab the attention of your audience and make them want to read more. Use power words, numbers, and emotional triggers in your headlines to make them compelling.

4. Tell a story: People love stories, and storytelling is an effective way to engage your audience. Use real-life examples, anecdotes, and narratives to make your content more relatable and engaging.

5. Use visuals: Visuals are an essential component of engaging content. Use images, videos, and infographics to make your content more visually appealing and easier to understand.

6. Make it interactive: Interactive content, such as quizzes, polls, and surveys, are highly engaging and can keep your audience hooked. They also provide valuable insights into your audience's preferences and opinions.

7. Keep it concise and to the point: Attention spans are short, and people are bombarded with information daily. Keep your content concise and to the point, and make sure it provides value to your audience.

By following these tips, you can create engaging content that resonates with your audience, builds your brand, and achieves high-end results.

WHY ENGAGING YOUR COSTUMER WITH HIGH-END CONTENT IS IMPORTANT

Engaging your customers with high-end content is important for several reasons:

1. Building Trust: When you provide high-quality content, you're not just selling a product or service, you're building trust with your customers. Customers are more likely to trust and buy from a brand that provides valuable, informative, and engaging content.

2. Brand Awareness: High-quality content can help your brand reach a larger audience, increasing brand awareness and visibility. When people share your content, it can help to further spread the word about your brand and what you have to offer.

3. Establishing Authority: By providing high-quality content, you establish yourself as an authority in your industry. Customers are more likely to trust and rely on a brand that has demonstrated expertise and knowledge in their field.

4. Increased Engagement: High-quality content is more likely to be shared, liked, and commented on, increasing engagement with your audience. This can help to build a loyal following and ultimately drive more sales.

5. Search Engine Optimization: High-quality content can also help to improve your search engine rankings, making it easier for potential customers to find you online. This is because

search engines prioritize content that is relevant, informative, and engaging.

Overall, engaging your customers with high-end content is essential for building trust, establishing authority, increasing brand awareness, and ultimately driving sales.

USING SOCIAL MEDIA TO DRIVE TRAFFIC TO YOUR WEBSITE

Using social media to drive traffic to your website can be an effective way to increase your online presence and attract new visitors. Here are some tips on how to use social media to drive traffic to your website:

1. Share your website URL: Share your website URL on your social media profiles, so your followers can easily find your website.
2. Post engaging content: Post engaging content on your social media profiles that will encourage your followers to click through to your website.

Make sure your posts are relevant to your website and your target audience.

3. Use images and videos: Visual content like images and videos tend to get more engagement on social media than text-only posts. Use visually appealing images or videos to draw attention to your website.

4. Use hashtags: Hashtags can help increase the visibility of your social media posts. Use relevant hashtags that are related to your website or niche to reach a wider audience.

5. Engage with your followers: Engage with your followers on social media by responding to comments and messages. Building a relationship with your followers can help drive traffic to your website.

6. Run social media ads: Running social media ads can help you reach a larger audience and drive more traffic to your website. Make sure your ads are targeted to the right audience and include a clear call-to-action to encourage clicks.

Overall, using social media to drive traffic to your website requires consistent effort and engagement. By posting engaging content, using visuals, and building relationships with your followers, you can increase your website traffic and online presence.

WHY THE USE OF SOCIAL MEDIA TO DRIVE TRAFFIC TO YOUR WEBSITE

Using social media to drive traffic to your website can be an effective strategy to increase your online presence and reach a wider audience. Here are some reasons why:

1. Increases brand awareness: By sharing your website content on social media, you can increase brand awareness and reach a larger audience. When people see your content on social media and click through to your website, they become more familiar with your brand and are more likely to remember it.

2. Boosts website traffic: Social media is a great way to attract more visitors to your website. By sharing links to your website content on social media, you can drive traffic back to your website and increase the number of page views.

3. Improves search engine rankings: Social media shares and engagement can help improve your website's search engine rankings. When people share your content on social media, it signals to search engines that your content is valuable and relevant, which can improve your search engine ranking.

4. Increases engagement: Social media can be an excellent way to engage with your audience and encourage them to interact with your content. When you share your content on social media, people can leave comments, ask questions, and share their own thoughts, which can create a sense of community and help to build relationships with your audience.

Overall, social media is a powerful tool that can help you reach a wider audience, drive more traffic to your website, and improve your online visibility.

WHY WE MUST BE CAREFUL OF USING SOCIAL MEDIA TO DRIVE TRAFFIC TO YOUR WEBSITE

There are several reasons why you must be careful when using social media to drive traffic to your website. Here are a few:

1. False or Misleading Claims: Social media platforms are not known for their accuracy, and there is a significant risk that false or misleading claims can be made. Such claims can harm the credibility of your website and, in some cases, lead to legal consequences.

2. Dependence on Social Media: Relying on social media for traffic can be risky because it is a constantly evolving medium. Social media platforms can change their algorithms or

introduce new rules and regulations that can impact your website's reach and engagement. This can lead to a sudden drop in traffic or even a complete loss of your social media following.

3. Limited Control: When using social media to drive traffic, you have limited control over the user experience. Users can get distracted or lose interest quickly, and it can be challenging to keep them engaged with your content or site. Additionally, social media platforms can remove your content or restrict your account without warning, further limiting your control.

4. Limited Reach: While social media can be an effective way to reach a broad audience, it can also limit your reach. Social media platforms tend to favor paid advertising and promoted content, meaning that organic reach can be limited.

5. Lack of Diversification: Relying solely on social media for traffic can limit your ability to diversify your traffic sources. Diversification is

crucial for the long-term success of your website, as it helps reduce your dependence on any one source of traffic.

In conclusion, while social media can be a valuable tool for driving traffic to your website, it is essential to approach it with caution and be mindful of its limitations. Diversifying your traffic sources and focusing on creating high-quality, engaging content can help mitigate some of the risks associated with social media marketing.

Chapter Eight

CHAPTER EIGHT

SEO AND CONTENT MARKETING

SEO (Search Engine Optimization) and Content Marketing are two related but distinct strategies used in digital marketing to improve website visibility and attract more organic traffic.

SEO involves optimizing website content and structure to improve search engine rankings and visibility in search engine results pages (SERPs). The goal is to make the website more appealing to search engines and help it appear higher in the organic search results. SEO techniques include keyword research, on-page optimization (e.g., optimizing page titles, meta descriptions, and content), link building, and technical optimization (e.g., optimizing website speed, mobile responsiveness, and security).

Content Marketing, on the other hand, focuses on creating and distributing valuable, relevant, and consistent content to attract and retain a clearly-defined audience and ultimately drive profitable customer action. The goal is to create content that appeals to the target audience and helps build brand authority and awareness. Content marketing techniques include blogging, video marketing, social media marketing, email marketing, and whitepapers.

While SEO and Content Marketing are distinct strategies, they often overlap and work together to achieve common goals. For example, high-quality content can attract backlinks, which can improve the website's SEO rankings. Likewise, SEO optimization can help increase the visibility of content and drive more traffic to it. Overall, both SEO and Content Marketing are critical components of a comprehensive digital marketing strategy.

IMPORTANT OF SEO AND CONTENT MARKETING IN BUSINESS

SEO (Search Engine Optimization) and content marketing are both important for businesses in different ways.

SEO helps businesses to improve their website's visibility and ranking in search engine results pages (SERPs) for relevant keywords and phrases. This means that when people search for information related to your business, your website will be more likely to appear at the top of search results, which can lead to more traffic, leads, and ultimately sales.

Content marketing, on the other hand, is all about creating valuable and relevant content that attracts and engages your target audience. This can include blog posts, videos, social media content, and more. The goal is to create content that not only educates and informs your audience but also establishes your brand as a thought leader in your industry.

When combined, SEO and content marketing can have a powerful impact on a business. By optimizing your content for search engines, you can increase its visibility and attract more traffic to your website. And by creating high-quality, engaging content, you can keep visitors on your site longer and build relationships with your audience.

In short, SEO helps people find your content, while content marketing helps keep them engaged and interested in your brand. By investing in both strategies, businesses can increase their online visibility, build brand awareness, and ultimately drive more leads and sales.

HOW TO OPTIMIZE YOUR WEBSITE FOR SEARCH ENGINES VISIBILITIES

Optimizing your website for search engines is crucial for increasing visibility and driving traffic to your site. Here are some tips to help you optimize your website for search engines:

1. Research keywords: Conduct keyword research to identify the words and phrases people use to search for the products or services you offer. Use keyword research tools like Google Keyword Planner or Ahrefs to find the right keywords.

2. Use keywords in title tags and meta descriptions: Include your primary keyword in the title tag and meta description of your website pages. This helps search engines understand the content of your page and improves your chances of ranking for relevant searches.

3. Create high-quality content: Write high-quality content that is informative and relevant to your target audience. Use your primary and secondary keywords in the content naturally, and avoid keyword stuffing.

4. Optimize images: Use descriptive filenames and alt tags for your images. This helps search engines understand what the image is about and improves your chances of ranking for relevant searches.

5. Use internal linking: Internal linking helps search engines understand the structure of your website and the relationship between pages. Use descriptive anchor text for internal links and link to relevant pages.

6. Make your website mobile-friendly: More and more people are using mobile devices to browse the internet. Make sure your website is mobile-friendly and loads quickly on mobile devices.

7. Improve website speed: A fast website improves the user experience and can improve your search

engine rankings. Use tools like Google PageSpeed Insights to identify issues that are slowing down your website.

8. Build high-quality backlinks: Backlinks from high-quality websites can improve your search engine rankings. Reach out to other websites in your industry and ask for backlinks.

9. Use social media: Social media can drive traffic to your website and improve your search engine rankings. Share your content on social media and engage with your followers.

By following these tips, you can optimize your website for search engines and improve your visibility and traffic.

CONTENT MARKETING AND BRAND BUILDING

Content marketing and brand building are closely related strategies that businesses use to increase brand awareness, engagement, and loyalty among their target audience.

Content marketing involves creating and distributing valuable, relevant, and consistent content to attract and retain a clearly-defined audience, ultimately driving profitable customer action. The goal of content marketing is to establish the business as a thought leader and trusted authority in its industry by providing educational and informative content that solves problems, answers questions, and addresses the pain points of its target audience.

Brand building, on the other hand, is the process of creating and promoting a brand image and identity that resonates with its target audience. It involves developing a unique brand voice, personality, and visual identity that conveys the business's values, mission, and vision, and differentiates it from its competitors. Brand building aims to create a strong emotional connection between the brand and its customers, building brand loyalty, and increasing customer retention.

Content marketing is a powerful tool for brand building, as it allows businesses to create content that aligns with their brand values and messaging, and reinforces their brand identity. By producing high-quality, valuable content consistently, businesses can establish themselves as thought leaders and experts in their industry, increasing brand awareness and loyalty among their target audience.

In summary, content marketing and brand building are interdependent strategies that work together to help businesses establish a strong brand identity, increase brand awareness, and build long-term customer relationships.

HOW TO CREATE HIGH-QUALITY CONTENT

Creating high-quality content requires a combination of several factors, including research, writing skills, and attention to detail. Here are some tips to help you create high-quality content:

1. Understand your audience: To create content that resonates with your audience, you need to understand their needs, interests, and pain points. Spend time researching your target audience and create content that speaks directly to them.

2. Conduct thorough research: High-quality content is based on thorough research. Before you start writing, spend time researching your topic, and make sure that you have a deep understanding of the subject matter.

3. Use a clear structure: A clear and logical structure helps to make your content easy to read and understand. Use headings,

subheadings, and bullet points to break up your content and make it more scannable.

4. Write in an engaging style: Writing in an engaging and conversational style can help to keep your readers interested and engaged. Use simple language, avoid jargon, and try to inject your personality into your writing.

5. Edit and proofread: Editing and proofreading are essential to ensure that your content is error-free and easy to read. Take the time to read through your content carefully, checking for spelling and grammar errors, and ensuring that your writing is clear and concise.

6. Use visuals: Including visuals such as images, videos, and infographics can help to break up your content and make it more engaging. Visuals can also help to illustrate complex ideas and make your content easier to understand.

7. Aim for originality: Creating original content can help to set your content apart from the competition. Try to bring a unique perspective

or approach to your content, and avoid simply rehashing existing ideas.

By following these tips, you can create high-quality content that engages your audience and helps to establish your authority in your field.

HOW TO USE CONTENT MARKETING TO DRIVE TRAFFIC AND BUILD YOUR BRAND

Content marketing is a powerful strategy for driving traffic to your website and building your brand. Here are some tips to help you use content marketing effectively:

1. Define your target audience: Before you start creating content, you need to understand who your target audience is. Identify their needs, interests, and pain points, and create content that speaks directly to them.

2. Develop a content strategy: Develop a content strategy that aligns with your business goals and target audience. Decide on the types of content you will create, the topics you will cover, and how you will distribute your content.

3. Create high-quality content: Create content that is informative, engaging, and valuable to your audience. Use a mix of formats, such as blog

posts, infographics, videos, and podcasts, to keep your content fresh and interesting.

4. Optimize your content for search engines: Use relevant keywords and optimize your content for search engines to make it easier for your audience to find your content. This will help to drive more traffic to your website.

5. Promote your content: Share your content on social media, email newsletters, and other channels to reach a wider audience. Engage with your audience by responding to comments and questions.

6. Measure your results: Track your content marketing efforts using analytics tools to see what is working and what is not. Use this information to refine your content strategy and improve your results over time.

7. Build relationships with influencers: Identify influencers in your niche and build relationships with them. Collaborate on content and promote each other's work to reach a wider audience.

By following these tips, you can use content marketing to drive traffic to your website, build your brand, and establish yourself as an authority in your niche.

WHY YOU MUST USE CONTENT MARKETING TO DRIVE TRAFFIC AND BUILD BRAND TO YOUR BUSINESS

Content marketing is an effective way to attract and engage your target audience, drive traffic to your website, and build brand awareness. Here are some reasons why:

1. Attracting and engaging your target audience: By creating valuable content that speaks to your audience's needs and interests, you can attract them to your website or social media profiles. Through relevant and engaging content, you can build trust and establish yourself as an authority in your industry, which can lead to more conversions and long-term customers.

2. Driving traffic to your website: Content marketing is a powerful tool for driving traffic to your website. By creating quality content that is optimized for search engines, you can improve your search engine rankings and attract more organic traffic to your site. Additionally, by promoting your content through social media and other channels, you can increase visibility and drive more traffic to your website.

3. Building brand awareness: By consistently producing and distributing high-quality content, you can build brand awareness and establish your brand as a leader in your industry. Your content can help your audience understand your brand values, products or services, and unique selling points, which can lead to increased brand recognition and loyalty.

In short, content marketing can help you attract and engage your target audience, drive traffic to your website, and build brand awareness, all of which are essential for the success of your business.

Chapter Nine

CHAPTER NINE

BUILDING SUCCESSFUL ONLINE BUSINESS

Building a successful online business requires careful planning, strategic execution, and continuous adaptation to changing market trends. Here are some steps to follow:

1. Define your niche: Identify your target audience, their needs, and the products or services that would best serve them. Conduct market research to understand the competition and to find gaps in the market that you can fill.

2. Develop a business plan: Outline your business model, revenue streams, marketing strategy, and financial projections. This plan will guide your decision-making and help you stay focused on your goals.

3. Create a brand identity: Develop a brand name, logo, and visual style that reflects your values and resonates with your target audience.

Consistency in branding across all channels (website, social media, packaging, etc.) will build brand recognition and trust.

4. Build a website: Your website is the face of your business, so invest in a well-designed, user-friendly website that showcases your products or services and makes it easy for customers to make purchases. Make sure your website is optimized for search engines and mobile devices.

5. Establish a social media presence: Identify the social media channels where your target audience is active and create profiles for your business. Use social media to engage with your audience, build brand awareness, and drive traffic to your website.

6. Develop a content strategy: Create valuable and engaging content (blog posts, videos, infographics, etc.) that educates and entertains your target audience. Share this content on your

website and social media channels to attract and retain customers.

7. Implement an email marketing strategy: Collect email addresses from your website visitors and customers, and use email marketing to keep them informed about your business, promote new products or services, and offer special deals.

8. Implement a sales strategy: Use data and analytics to understand your customers' buying behavior and tailor your sales strategy accordingly. Offer personalized recommendations and incentives to encourage repeat purchases and referrals.

9. Continuously evaluate and improve: Monitor your website traffic, social media engagement, email open rates, and sales data to identify areas for improvement. Use this data to adapt your marketing and sales strategies and to stay ahead of the competition.

Building a successful online business is a challenging but rewarding process that requires dedication, hard work, and a willingness to learn and adapt. By following these steps and staying focused on your goals, you can build a thriving online business that meets the needs of your target audience and drives sustainable growth.

WHY YOU NEED TO BUILD A SUCCESSFUL ONLINE BUSINESS

There are several reasons why building a successful online business can be beneficial:

1. Flexibility: An online business allows you to work from anywhere, as long as you have an internet connection. This can give you the freedom to work from home, a coffee shop, or even while traveling.

2. Cost-effectiveness: Starting an online business can be more cost-effective than starting a traditional brick-and-mortar business. You may not need to invest in a physical location, pay rent, or hire a large staff.

3. Reach: The internet allows you to reach a global audience, which can increase your potential customer base significantly.

4. Scalability: Online businesses can be easily scaled to accommodate growth. With the right systems in place, you can handle more

customers without needing to expand your physical space or hire additional staff.

5. Income potential: A successful online business can provide you with a substantial income. With the right product or service, marketing strategy, and business model, you can generate significant revenue.

In building a successful online business can provide you with flexibility, cost-effectiveness, global reach, scalability, and income potential.

TYPE OF SUCCESSFUL ONLINE BUSINESS

There are many types of successful online businesses that have emerged in recent years. Here are a few examples:

1. E-commerce: This includes online stores that sell products directly to consumers. Examples of successful e-commerce businesses include Amazon, eBay, and Shopify.

2. Subscription-based businesses: This model involves charging customers a recurring fee for access to a product or service. Examples of successful subscription-based businesses include Netflix, Spotify, and Birchbox.

3. Online marketplaces: These platforms connect buyers and sellers, allowing them to transact with each other. Examples of successful online marketplaces include Etsy, Airbnb, and Uber.

4. Digital products: This includes businesses that create and sell digital products such as software, e-books, courses, and templates. Examples of

successful digital product businesses include Canva, Coursera, and Udemy.

5. Affiliate marketing: This model involves promoting other people's products or services and earning a commission on each sale. Examples of successful affiliate marketing businesses include Amazon Associates and ShareASale.

These are just a few examples of successful online business models. Ultimately, the key to success is to find a business model that meets a real need in the market and provides value to customers.

HIGH PAYING ONLINE BUSINESS

There are many high paying online business opportunities, but success in any of these ventures depends on several factors including market demand, competition, marketing strategies, and more. Here are some online business ideas that have the potential to generate high profits:

1. E-commerce Store: Starting an online store selling products that are in high demand is a great way to earn money. You can either create your own products or source them from a manufacturer or wholesaler.

2. Affiliate Marketing: This involves promoting other people's products and earning a commission for each sale made through your unique referral link. To be successful in affiliate marketing, you need to build a strong online presence and have a loyal audience.

3. Online Courses: If you have expertise in a particular field, you can create online courses

and sell them through platforms like Udemy or Teachable.

4. Dropshipping: This is a business model where you don't need to hold inventory, as you source products from a supplier who handles all the storage, shipping, and delivery. You only need to create a website, promote the products, and earn a commission for each sale made.

5. Digital Products: You can create digital products like eBooks, software, and online tools and sell them on platforms like Amazon or your own website.

Remember, any online business requires hard work, dedication, and a willingness to learn and adapt. You also need to have a good understanding of your target audience, industry trends, and marketing techniques to succeed.

PRINCIPLES OF BUILDING A SUCCESSFUL ONLINE BUSINESS

Building a successful online business involves the following several principles that are essential for the growth and sustainability of the business. Some of the key principles include:

1. Identify a need: Successful online businesses typically identify a gap in the market or a problem that needs solving. They then create a product or service that meets that need or solves the problem.

2. Focus on user experience: User experience is crucial to the success of an online business. A successful online business ensures that its website is easy to navigate, its products or services are easy to find, and the checkout process is seamless.

3. Build a strong brand: A strong brand is essential for building trust and loyalty with customers. Successful online businesses invest in creating a

strong brand identity through consistent branding, messaging, and visual elements.

4. Embrace technology: Online businesses need to be up to date with the latest technology and trends to remain competitive. This includes utilizing social media, SEO, and other digital marketing techniques to reach a wider audience.

5. Build a loyal customer base: A successful online business focuses on building a loyal customer base by providing excellent customer service, offering incentives such as discounts and rewards, and creating a sense of community through social media and other channels.

6. Stay adaptable: Online businesses need to be adaptable to changing market conditions and trends. This means being willing to pivot or change course when necessary to stay relevant and competitive.

By following these principles, online businesses can increase their chances of success and achieve sustainable growth over time.

HOW TO REMAIN RELEVANT AND SUCCESSFUL IN AN ONLINE SPACE

To remain relevant and successful in an online space, here are some tips:

1. Stay up to date with the latest trends: Online trends are constantly changing, and it's important to keep up with them to remain relevant. Stay informed by following industry blogs, news sources, and social media accounts.

2. Provide value to your audience: People visit websites and social media accounts to get something of value, whether that's information, entertainment, or inspiration. Make sure you provide that value to your audience consistently.

3. Engage with your audience: Engage with your audience regularly through comments,

messages, and other forms of interaction. This will help build a relationship with them and create a loyal following.

4. Use data to inform your strategy: Use analytics tools to track your website and social media performance, and use that data to inform your content strategy and improve your online presence.

5. Collaborate with others: Collaborate with other online influencers, bloggers, and brands to expand your reach and bring new audiences to your content.

6. Be authentic and transparent: Authenticity and transparency are important to online audiences. Be genuine in your interactions and transparent about any sponsored content or partnerships.

7. Keep evolving: Online spaces are always changing, and it's important to adapt and evolve to stay relevant. Continuously test new strategies and tactics to see what works best for you and your audience.

SETTING GOALS AND STAYING ORGANIZED

Setting goals and staying organized are two essential skills for success in any area of life, whether personal or professional. Goals provide direction and purpose, while staying organized helps to manage time, resources, and achieve those goals efficiently. In this analysis, we will discuss the importance of setting goals and staying organized, their benefits, and some practical tips for developing these skills.

Importance of Setting Goals: Setting goals is critical for achieving success in any area of life. Goals provide direction, focus, and motivation for individuals, teams, or organizations. They help us to clarify what we want to achieve and determine the steps required to get there. Without clear goals, we may lack direction, become easily distracted, and lose sight of what we want to accomplish.

Benefits of Setting Goals: Setting goals offers several benefits, including:

1. Clarity: Goals provide clarity on what you want to achieve, why you want to achieve it, and how you plan to accomplish it.

2. Focus: Goals help to focus your efforts and resources towards achieving the desired outcome.

3. Motivation: Goals provide motivation by creating a sense of purpose and a clear target to work towards.

4. Measurement: Goals provide a clear way to measure progress and success, allowing you to assess whether you are on track or need to adjust your approach.

Importance of Staying Organized: Staying organized is essential for achieving success in any area of life. Organization allows us to manage our time, resources, and tasks efficiently, reducing stress and increasing productivity. Without organization, we may waste time and effort on unnecessary tasks, miss deadlines, and struggle to achieve our goals.

Benefits of Staying Organized: Staying organized offers several benefits, including:

1. Increased Productivity: Staying organized helps to manage time efficiently, allowing us to accomplish more in less time.
2. Reduced Stress: Being organized reduces stress by providing clarity, reducing the feeling of overwhelm, and helping to prioritize tasks.
3. Improved Time Management: Staying organized allows us to manage our time effectively, ensuring that we prioritize tasks and meet deadlines.
4. Better Decision Making: Being organized allows us to access important information quickly, facilitating better decision-making.

Tips for Setting Goals: To set effective goals, consider the following tips:

1. Be Specific: Goals should be specific and measurable, defining exactly what you want to achieve.

2. Make Them Attainable: Goals should be challenging but attainable, ensuring that they are realistic and achievable.

3. Make Them Relevant: Goals should be relevant to your overall purpose and aligned with your values and priorities.

4. Set a Deadline: Goals should have a specific deadline, providing a sense of urgency and helping to prioritize tasks.

Tips for Staying Organized: To stay organized, consider the following tips:

1. Prioritize Tasks: Prioritize tasks based on importance and urgency, ensuring that you focus on high-priority tasks first.

2. Use a Planner: Use a planner or a to-do list to track tasks, deadlines, and appointments.

3. Keep Your Space Tidy: Keep your workspace organized and clutter-free, reducing distractions and increasing focus.

4. Automate Tasks: Use automation tools to reduce the time and effort required to complete repetitive tasks.

In conclusion, setting goals and staying organized are essential skills for success in any area of life. Goals provide direction and purpose, while staying organized helps to manage time, resources, and achieve those goals efficiently. By following the tips provided above, you can develop these skills and achieve success in your personal and professional life.

CONTINUALLY LEARNING AND IMPROVEMENT

Continual learning and improvement is the process of constantly acquiring new knowledge and skills, and applying that knowledge to improve oneself or a particular area of interest. This concept is important in many aspects of life, from personal growth to professional development. In this analysis, we will explore the benefits and challenges of continual learning and improvement, as well as some strategies for achieving success.

BENEFITS OF CONTINUAL LEARNING AND IMPROVEMENT

1. Personal Growth: Continual learning and improvement can help individuals to grow and develop as people. It can increase self-awareness and self-confidence, as well as broaden horizons and provide new opportunities for personal fulfillment.

2. Professional Development: Continual learning and improvement is essential for success in many professions. It can help individuals stay up-to-date with the latest developments in their field, as well as acquire new skills and knowledge that can lead to career advancement.

3. Innovation: Continual learning and improvement can also lead to innovation and creativity. By constantly seeking out new information and experiences, individuals can develop unique perspectives and ideas that can lead to breakthroughs and advancements in various fields.

4. Adaptability: Continual learning and improvement can help individuals adapt to changing circumstances and environments. It can also help individuals develop resilience and the ability to overcome challenges.

CHALLENGES OF CONTINUAL LEARNING AND IMPROVEMENT

1. Time: Continual learning and improvement can be time-consuming. It can be difficult to find the time to pursue new knowledge and skills, particularly for individuals with busy schedules.

2. Cost: Some forms of continual learning and improvement, such as formal education or training programs, can be expensive. This can be a barrier for individuals who cannot afford to invest in these resources.

3. Motivation: Continual learning and improvement requires motivation and discipline. It can be easy to become complacent or distracted, particularly if the benefits of continual learning are not immediately apparent.

4. Overload: Continual learning and improvement can also lead to information overload. With so much information available, it can be difficult to

know where to focus one's efforts and how to prioritize learning objectives.

STRATEGIES FOR CONTINUAL LEARNING AND IMPROVEMENT

1. Set Goals: Setting specific, achievable goals can help individuals stay focused and motivated. Goals can also help individuals measure progress and track their success.

2. Seek Out Resources: There are many resources available for continual learning and improvement, from books and articles to online courses and training programs. By seeking out these resources, individuals can find the information and guidance they need to succeed.

3. Network: Networking with peers and colleagues can provide valuable opportunities for learning and growth. By sharing knowledge and experiences, individuals can broaden their perspectives and learn from others.

4. Take Breaks: It is important to take breaks and allow time for reflection and assimilation of new information. This can help individuals avoid burnout and maintain a healthy balance between learning and other aspects of life.

Continual learning and improvement is an essential component of personal and professional growth. While there are challenges associated with this process, the benefits are numerous, and there are many strategies individuals can use to achieve success. By committing to a process of continual learning and improvement, individuals can enhance their skills, broaden their horizons, and achieve their goals.

Chapter Ten

CHAPTER TEN

SUCCESS

Success is the achievement of a goal or objective that is desired. It can be measured in various ways, such as wealth, power, status, personal fulfillment, or happiness. Success is often the result of hard work, persistence, dedication, and making the most of opportunities that come your way.

However, success can mean different things to different people. For some, success may mean achieving financial stability, while for others it may mean having a happy family life or making a positive impact on the world. Ultimately, success is subjective and varies from person to person, and it is up to each individual to define what success means to them and work towards achieving it.

Success can be measured in various ways, such as financial prosperity, career advancement, personal fulfillment, social recognition, or simply overcoming a challenging obstacle. Success can also involve a combination of these factors and may be subjective to individual values and aspirations. Ultimately, success can be seen as a state of achievement or accomplishment in which an individual's efforts have resulted in a positive outcome.

TIPS FOR SUCCESS

Here are some tips for success that can be applied in various aspects of life:

1. Set clear goals: Define your goals and establish a plan on how to achieve them. Write down your goals and break them down into smaller, achievable steps.

2. Prioritize your tasks: Focus on the most important tasks and prioritize them accordingly. This will help you to avoid procrastination and increase your productivity.

3. Develop good habits: Form good habits such as regular exercise, healthy eating, and getting enough sleep. These habits will help you maintain your physical and mental well-being.

4. Stay organized: Keep your work and personal life organized. Use tools such as calendars, to-do lists, and reminders to stay on top of your tasks.

5. Continuous learning: Stay curious and continue to learn. Read books, attend seminars, and take courses to improve your knowledge and skills.

6. Stay positive: Maintain a positive mindset and focus on the positive aspects of situations. This will help you to overcome challenges and maintain a healthy outlook on life.

7. Surround yourself with positive people: Surround yourself with people who encourage and support your goals. These individuals will help you to stay motivated and on track.

8. Take calculated risks: Take calculated risks and step outside of your comfort zone. This will help you to grow and develop as an individual.

9. Persevere: Be persistent in the pursuit of your goals. Keep going even when faced with obstacles and setbacks.

10. Take care of yourself: Take care of yourself physically, mentally, and emotionally. Practice self-care and take time to relax and recharge.

TIPS AND TRICKS TO HELP YOU SUCCEED IN THE ONLINE MARKETPLACE

Certainly, here are some tips and tricks that can help you succeed in the online marketplace:

1. Identify Your Target Audience: Knowing your target audience and their needs is crucial to succeeding in the online marketplace. It will help you tailor your products or services to their preferences and deliver a more personalized experience.

2. Establish a Strong Brand Identity: Your brand is your identity online. Establishing a strong brand identity will help you stand out in the crowded online marketplace. Make sure your brand values, messaging, and visual identity are consistent across all your online channels.

3. Build a Professional Website: Your website is your storefront in the online marketplace. Make sure it is visually appealing, easy to navigate, and optimized for search engines. Ensure that

the content is clear, concise, and relevant to your target audience.

4. Invest in SEO: Search engine optimization (SEO) is crucial for driving traffic to your website. Optimize your website content for relevant keywords and make sure your site is mobile-friendly and fast-loading.

5. Leverage Social Media: Social media platforms are a powerful tool for reaching and engaging with your target audience. Choose the social media channels that are most relevant to your target audience and create engaging content that resonates with them.

6. Offer Exceptional Customer Service: Customer service is a key differentiator in the online marketplace. Respond to customer queries promptly and offer personalized solutions to their problems.

7. Offer Competitive Pricing: The online marketplace is highly competitive. Offering

competitive pricing can help you attract more customers and drive sales.

8. Use Analytics to Monitor Performance: Use web analytics tools to track your website's performance and identify areas for improvement. Use this data to refine your online strategy and optimize your online channels.

9. Continuously Innovate: The online marketplace is constantly evolving. Continuously innovate and stay ahead of the curve by keeping up with the latest trends and technologies in your industry.

ANALYSIS OF TIME EFFECTIVENESS TO BUILDING A STRONG SUPPORT SYSTEM

Building a strong support system can be a crucial factor in achieving success in various aspects of life, including personal and professional endeavors. However, the time effectiveness of building such a system can vary depending on several factors. In this analysis, we will explore these factors and their impact on the time effectiveness of building a strong support system.

1. Availability of Resources: The availability of resources such as time, money, and energy can significantly impact the time effectiveness of building a strong support system. If one has limited resources, it may take longer to establish a support system as they may need to prioritize other commitments or find ways to stretch their resources to invest in building their network.

2. Networking Skills: One's networking skills can also play a vital role in the time effectiveness of building a strong support system. Individuals who possess excellent networking skills and are comfortable making new connections may find it easier to expand their network and build a strong support system more quickly. On the other hand, those who struggle with networking

may take longer to establish meaningful connections and build a robust support system.

3. Personal and Professional Goals: The nature of one's personal and professional goals can also affect the time effectiveness of building a strong support system. For instance, if one's goals require a broad network of contacts or specific expertise, they may need to invest more time in networking and building a support system. In contrast, if their goals do not require extensive networking, they may be able to establish a support system relatively quickly.

4. Existing Relationships: The strength and depth of one's existing relationships can also impact the time effectiveness of building a strong support system. Individuals who already have a solid network of friends, family, and professional contacts may find it easier to leverage these existing relationships and build a strong support system more quickly. On the other hand, those who lack existing relationships

may need to invest more time in making new connections.

5. Consistency and Persistence: Consistency and persistence in building a strong support system can significantly impact its time effectiveness. Those who are consistent and persistent in networking and building relationships are more likely to make progress and establish a strong support system quickly. Conversely, those who are inconsistent or give up easily may find it challenging to build a support system.

The time effectiveness of building a strong support system can vary depending on several factors, including the availability of resources, networking skills, personal and professional goals, existing relationships, and consistency and persistence. It is important to understand these factors and tailor one's approach to building a support system accordingly. With the right mindset, approach, and investment, building a strong support system can be a fulfilling and rewarding journey.

STRATEGY TO BUILDING A STRONG SUPPORT SYSTEM AND EFFECTIVE TIME MANAGEMENT

Building a strong support system and effective time management are two essential components of a successful life. Here are some strategies to achieve both:

1. Identify your priorities: Determine what is most important to you and prioritize your time accordingly. Make a list of your goals and break them down into smaller, more manageable tasks.

2. Create a schedule: Develop a daily or weekly schedule that outlines your activities, deadlines, and commitments. Include time for self-care and relaxation.

3. Set boundaries: Learn to say "no" to requests or commitments that do not align with your priorities. Setting boundaries will help you manage your time more effectively and prevent burnout.

4. Delegate tasks: If possible, delegate tasks to others who are capable and willing to help. This will free up time for you to focus on your top priorities.

5. Build a support system: Surround yourself with positive, supportive people who share your values and goals. Join clubs or organizations related to your interests or career.

6. Communicate effectively: Be clear and direct in your communication with others. Make sure that you express your needs and expectations clearly, and listen actively to others.

7. Stay organized: Keep track of important information and deadlines using a planner, calendar, or digital tool. This will help you avoid last-minute crises and reduce stress.

8. Take breaks: Remember to take breaks throughout the day to recharge your batteries and maintain your focus. Regular breaks can actually improve your productivity and overall well-being.

By following these strategies, you can build a strong support system and manage your time effectively, leading to greater success and fulfillment in all areas of your life.

Effective time management and building a strong support system are two important aspects that can help you achieve success in your personal and professional life. Here are some tips on how to manage your time effectively and build a strong support system:

1. Prioritize your tasks: Make a to-do list and prioritize your tasks based on their importance and urgency. Focus on completing the most important tasks first, and then move on to the less important ones.

2. Set realistic goals: Set realistic goals for yourself and break them down into smaller, manageable tasks. This will help you stay motivated and focused.

3. Use a calendar or planner: Use a calendar or planner to schedule your tasks and appointments. This will help you stay organized and ensure that you don't miss any important deadlines.

4. Learn to say no: It's important to learn to say no to things that aren't important or that will take up too much of your time. This will help you stay focused on your goals and priorities.

5. Delegate tasks: If possible, delegate tasks to others who are capable of doing them. This will free up your time and allow you to focus on more important tasks.

6. Build a strong support system: Surround yourself with people who support and encourage you. This could include family, friends, colleagues, or mentors.

7. Communicate effectively: Communicate your goals and needs to your support system. This will help them understand what you're trying to achieve and how they can best support you.

8. Be open to feedback: Be open to feedback from your support system. This can help you identify areas for improvement and make necessary changes to achieve your goals.

By following these tips, you can manage your time effectively and build a strong support system to help you achieve success in your personal and professional life.

FOCUSED ON ACHIEVING YOUR GOALS

1. Set clear and specific goals: When setting your goals, make sure they are clear, specific, and measurable. Having specific goals can help you stay focused and motivated.

2. Break down larger goals into smaller, manageable steps: This can make the goal feel less daunting and easier to achieve. Each small step you take can give you a sense of progress and accomplishment, which can help keep you motivated.

3. Stay organized: Keep track of your progress and plan your tasks in advance. This can help you stay on track and avoid feeling overwhelmed.

4. Prioritize your tasks: Determine which tasks are the most important and make sure to tackle those first. This can help you avoid procrastination and keep you moving towards your goals.

5. Stay motivated: Find ways to stay motivated, whether it's by visualizing your success, reminding yourself of your end goal, or rewarding yourself for progress made. Keeping a positive attitude can go a long way in helping you achieve your goals.

Remember, achieving your goals takes time, effort, and persistence. By staying focused and following these tips, you can increase your chances of success.

HOW TO STAY FOCUSED AND ACHIEVING YOUR GOALS

Staying focused on achieving your goals can be a challenging task, but it is essential if you want to succeed in life. Here are some strategies and techniques that you can use to help you stay focused on your goals:

1. Define your goals clearly: The first step towards staying focused on your goals is to define them

clearly. Be specific about what you want to achieve, why you want to achieve it, and how you plan to achieve it. Write down your goals and break them down into smaller, more manageable tasks.

2. Create a plan: Once you have defined your goals, create a plan of action. Set deadlines for each task and prioritize them according to their importance. Make a schedule and stick to it.

3. Eliminate distractions: To stay focused on your goals, you need to eliminate distractions. Turn off your phone, log out of social media, and find a quiet place to work. If you work in an environment with distractions, consider using noise-cancelling headphones or finding a different location to work.

4. Stay motivated: Motivation is key to staying focused on your goals. Remind yourself why you want to achieve your goals and visualize the end result. Celebrate your progress and reward yourself for achieving milestones.

5. Stay organized: Being organized can help you stay focused on your goals. Keep track of your progress and stay on top of your schedule. Use tools like calendars, to-do lists, and project management software to stay organized.

6. Focus on one thing at a time: Trying to multitask can be counterproductive. Instead, focus on one task at a time and give it your full attention. Once you have completed that task, move on to the next one.

7. Stay positive: Staying positive can help you stay focused on your goals. Believe in yourself and your ability to achieve your goals. Surround yourself with positive people who will support and encourage you.

8. Take breaks: Taking breaks can help you stay focused and avoid burnout. Take short breaks throughout the day to recharge and refocus your mind.

9. Learn from setbacks: Setbacks and failures are a natural part of the process. Instead of getting

discouraged, use them as an opportunity to learn and grow. Analyze what went wrong and use that knowledge to make improvements.

In conclusion, staying focused on your goals requires discipline, dedication, and hard work. By defining your goals clearly, creating a plan, eliminating distractions, staying motivated, staying organized, focusing on one thing at a time, staying positive, taking breaks, and learning from setbacks, you can stay on track and achieve your goals.

GENERAL OVERVIEW OF THE BOOK

"The Ultimate Guide to Making Money Online: Strategies and Tips for Success" is a comprehensive guidebook that explores various ways to earn money through the internet. These guide provides valuable insights into online business opportunities and strategies to generate income from them.

The guidebook starts by discussing the importance of having a clear goal and motivation for making money online. It also emphasizes the need to understand the online marketplace and how to effectively reach potential customers. It delves into different strategies such as affiliate marketing, selling digital products, and dropshipping.

The section on affiliate marketing covers how to choose the right products to promote, how to build an audience, and the importance of building trust with your audience. The guide also provides tips on how to leverage social media platforms to promote affiliate products and increase conversions.

The section on selling digital products discusses various digital products that one can create and sell, including ebooks, courses, and software. The authors provide tips on how to create high-quality digital products that people will be willing to pay for and how to market them effectively.

The section on dropshipping explains how to set up a successful dropshipping business, including how to choose the right niche, how to find reliable suppliers, and how to build a website that attracts customers.

The guidebook also covers other ways to make money online, such as freelance writing, virtual assisting, and online tutoring. It provides tips on how to find clients and build a successful online business in these fields.

Overall, "The Ultimate Guide to Making Money Online: Strategies and Tips for Success" is a valuable resource for anyone looking to generate income online. The guidebook provides practical advice and actionable strategies that can help beginners and experienced entrepreneurs alike succeed in the online marketplace.

www.ingramcontent.com/pod-product-compliance
Lightning Source LLC
Chambersburg PA
CBHW070528220526
45467CB00003B/897